T0114835

Mom's LOVE

The True Story of a Mother's Struggles
and a Son's Recovery and Redemption

CARIDAD

authorHOUSE®

AuthorHouse™
1663 Liberty Drive
Bloomington, IN 47403
www.authorhouse.com
Phone: 833-262-8899

Published by AuthorHouse 04/28/2021

ISBN: 978-1-6655-0688-5 (sc)
ISBN: 978-1-6655-0687-8 (e)

Library of Congress Control Number: 2020921976

Print information available on the last page.

CONTENTS

INTRODUCTION

This book was inspired behind bars, when all was lost, and the pain and suffering was unbearable, it was written with the purpose of giving hope to all the Mothers and family members of individuals that suffer from addiction and alcoholism, incarcerated, or on their way to destruction.

If reading this story, could change one readers path from being helpless and hopeless lost and dejected to being hopeful, aware and proud, then we have accomplished our goal.

We all have a story or know some body that has a story, this is our story from the goodness of a modest life, to the immorality brought by addiction and disfunction, then gaining back the goodness of the modest life and freedom from bondage, thanks to God's Mercy and the twelve steps program of recovery.

God knows I am not perfect and as a mother I tried my hardest to provide for my children. But one thing I did with vigorous efforts was to show all my children that there is a God, that he exists and that his forgiveness, mercy, grace and love endures forever, deeper, and even stronger than a mom's love for her children. May you find the answers to your troubles, like we have found in God, in this book.

CHAPTER 1

In His Addiction and Insanity

On Saturday morning, September 24, 2005, the sound of six gunshots from a .40-caliber Smith & Wesson filled the air of East 13 Street Hialeah Miami Florida. There was some heavy breathing and then a screeching scream of fear from the lady next door.

The Next-door neighbor stood frozen in shock at what was before her eyes. At approximately twenty feet to her left on her neighbor's porch there was a man slumped in a fetal position in a puddle of blood in broad daylight. Blood Flowed out of his side like a fountain. About ten feet away from the afflicted man stood another man. He wore black-and-red G-Unit Reeboks with black ankle socks. His black Dickies shorts were pulled down an inch so that only the waistband of his plaid boxers was exposed. He stood shirtless, arms hanging by his sides. In his left hand, he gripped a huge black-and-gray pistol. His index finger rested on its trigger.

Freeze the frame for a minute, please.

Oh yeah, there he is. His name is Angel . In his addiction and insanity, he's lost *everything*, including his mind.

There he stands, just twenty years old. He's so young, so handsome, so full of love and charisma, even if it doesn't seem that way. At this moment, you are meeting him at his worst. He is tired and weary. The pressures of this world on his shoulders have worn him down. He has so much potential. He is so smart but is such a fool for surrounding himself with the wrong crowd. He's a true sucker for love, always looking for love in all the wrong places. He thinks he knows it all. He's at his peak, making a lot of money for his age, providing for both his family and his wife's parents. He's a family man, married with two sons. He's always protective of his family and very low key. You could almost say he lives a double life. He has no legitimate profession because he only has an eighth-grade education. But one thing about Angel is that he can always accomplish anything that he puts his mind to. He is a go-getter who knows the streets and knows how to make something out of nothing. He is overall a good man with a humongous heart and great sense of humor. He is so funny; he's often told he even looks and acts like Adam Sandler.

I know him perfectly well, because you see, Angel is my son.

But look at him on that September morning in 2005; look at what he has done. His shoulders are slumped as if he has bad posture. His head is down. He's given up. He's exhausted from the fight. Although he has slain his assailant, he feels defeat deep down inside. If you could look into his big, brown, sorrow-filled eyes, you would feel his pain. You would feel his frustrations and the agitations of being born against all odds and being dealt a bad hand from the start. But he is a survivor; he is strong. He's made the best of our situation of poverty and struggle the only way he knows how. He's helped us make ends meet, and when he finally feels like he's caught a break, this tragedy takes place.

So, can you picture him? What do you see? He has been labeled and stereotyped with all types of horrendous titles, such as murderer, killer, thug, hoodlum, Mafioso, gangster, drug addict, alcoholic, drug dealer, and more.

It's easy for people to point the finger, criticize, and judge nowadays... you know, be all in the "Kool-Aid" When they don't even know the flavor. (referring to one who is spreading gossip of a false nature) Nobody in this world is perfect, not even one. Let he who has no sin cast the first stone. But remember, when you point your index finger, you have fingers pointing back at you: your pinky, ring finger, and middle finger. Don't spit up in the air, because it can fall back in your face. The man that you are looking at could be your child.

Do you want to know what I see when I look at him? I see my baby, my toddler, my little boy...and he's lost. He needs guidance; he needs God to redirect his path in life. Satan and his demons have tormented him long enough; it even seems as if they've gotten the best of him. Though the situation might look disastrous, Angel is entering the stages of what my program would describe as rock bottom. He needs help, he needs revival, but most of all to get him through all of this, he needs his mom's love.

CHAPTER 2

Born against All Odds

Before we get into the details leading up to what happened on the morning of mourning, I would like to give you somewhat of an understanding of this child of mine. He's abnormal! I wasn't supposed to get pregnant, because I was on birth control. I was religiously taking birth control pills while partying with Joseph, Angel's father. It was 1984, and we were two Cuban immigrants living it up in Miami, Florida.

We enjoyed our nights on the beach, indulging in parties, clubs, dancing, drinking alcohol and liquor, snorting a little cocaine, and living life to the fullest. I was completely oblivious to the fact that I was pregnant. This kid just slid in there, literally. Someway, somehow, he got in where he fit in and decided to comfortably reside in my womb, joining the party incognito.

I knew those cravings for Bacardi wine coolers weren't normal. After the absence of a few periods, I decided to visit my doctor. The necessary testing confirmed that I was pregnant. The doctor warned me of possible birth defects and retardation that could occur since I unknowingly continued taking the birth control pills after the baby had already been conceived. The doctor explained that these types of things happen, and I shouldn't be hard on myself because I had no possible way of knowing. He also suggested that I should consider having an abortion.

At this time, I had a three-year-old daughter, and I had just had an abortion a little after she turned two years old. I think I speak for a lot of women when I say that having an abortion takes a huge toll on a woman, mentally and physically. The pain and depression I experienced from killing my own child, my baby, is something I will live with for the rest of my life. It is so horrible. I've cried many nights and vowed that I would never do such a terrible thing ever again.

I couldn't help but feel appalled that the doctor suggested abortion so nonchalantly, as if we were talking about changing the oil or brakes in a car.

"No!" I exclaimed through tears. "Abortion is out of the question. If this baby is born with defects or retardation, I will take care of him or her for as long as I live, but I will not kill another one of my babies."

On the same of my birth date my son was born. I gave birth to a beautiful baby boy who weighed in at 7.5 pounds and was twenty-two inches long. He was perfect, with no birth defects at all. I counted all his fingers and toes, and the doctor and nurses checked him out too. He was as healthy as could be! His father wasn't there, but Angel had me and my family, and we wrapped him in our love. His birth was a joyous time for both of us, and from that day on, my son and I would always celebrate sharing our birthdays together. Thank God I didn't abort!

Although on the outside Angel seemed perfect, he was born with a sickness, a disease called alcoholism and addiction. It's in his genes, a disease inherited from his father and me. It's like a poison inside his veins, venom that silently subdues, unseen and unknown to the naked eye. Overall, Angel was born in Hialeah Hospital on April 11, 1985, against all odds.

CHAPTER 3

Morning of mourning

On September 24, 2005, at approximately four thirty in the morning, Angel sat alone at his dining room table. The whole house was quiet; everything was still. While everyone slept, he sat there restless, contemplating his life, his children's future, and even his own future. "How long will this last?" he asked himself in a whisper.

He glanced at his front window toward the front door and had a vision of the DEA or some type of SWAT-like authorities bursting in through the doors, geared up with tactical attire and with rifles aimed at him, screaming demands. The vision filled his mind—so alive, so real, and so vivid. He shook his head from side to side, trying to erase the thought, but instead another vision of "jack boys" (a term used for home-invading robbers) entered his mind. It was hard to tell the robbers and authorities apart because around this time, jack boys would dress up and impersonate the authorities to trick people into surrendering. By the time the mark realized the invaders weren't the authorities, it was too late. They'd probably already been disarmed and hogtied with tie wraps, and the jack boys would be pillaging the house, robbing everything. In certain cases, the jack boys would even slap and torture children or rape women in the mark's face to get extra information on hidden money or drugs.

Angel shook his head once more, trying to erase those thoughts from his mind; they were much more horrifying than the first thoughts had been. He glanced down at the huge black-and-gray Smith & Wesson .40 caliber that was gripped in his left hand and then glanced up at his blue

Springfield twelve-gauge pump that rested on top of the kitchen cabinet. He made a mental note that he would shoot it out with either one of them. He kissed his pistol and whispered, "Duly noted. Over my dead body—isn't that right, baby?" He smirked and looked away. His eyes landed on an open book sitting on his kitchen dinette table. It was a golden Gideon Bible with a red-ribbon marker and gold-trimmed pages.

He stood up and walked up to it. It was open to Psalm 23. He read it, and a rush of guilt and pain ran through him. He felt dirty and ashamed of what he had become. "What type of man am I?" he mentally questioned himself. "What type of fatherly example am I leading?" He had become the epitome of what he'd despised the most as a child. He was a manufacturer, distributor, and deliverer of controlled substances—the same controlled substances that tore apart his household and separated him from his father. He felt trapped. He was in too deep. He had only an eighth-grade education, and there was no job in his county that would pay him enough to cover all his expenses.

He couldn't go to school; there was no time. Who would run the dangerous business? He couldn't trust anyone. Where and how would the income come from to pay for everything? How long would this last? This time the question was directed toward God. If there is a God, Angel contemplated. Will I ever see heaven? he thought. Deep down, he knew he wouldn't. He had sold his soul to the devil in return for work, and if he was in this business, he belonged to Satan. He was Satan's slave, and he was doing the devil's work. He felt dead and numb inside. His wife and her family couldn't have cared about him, but if the money kept coming in, they kept sucking the life out of him like leeches.

Around eight thirty that morning, Angel went to get a haircut. When he got back home, he made his wife breakfast in bed out of gratitude for the good times they had the night before. He gave their two-month-old son a bottle and kissed them both. He then took his oldest son, two-year-old Angel Jr., downstairs. Angel made Junior chocolate milk and made fried egg sandwiches with cheesy bread for both. Shortly after they ate, Angel put the *Pirates of the Caribbean* movie in the DVD player with surround sound and sat Junior down in the living room on the black leather sofa. Angel took his shirt off and sat at the dining room table to roll up a blunt, when suddenly, they were both startled by the dogs barking and a loud banging on the door. Junior turned to his father and said, "Papi, the door." Angel stood up and walked over to look out the living room window.

Outside was a stranger about five feet nine, a number-two haircut all around. He had black-framed eyeglasses and a Rick Ross bin Laden beard. He wore a white tank top also known as a wife-beater top, blue jeans, and a pair of red-and-white Jordan sneakers. He was surrounded by Angel 's barking dogs: three Jack Russell terriers and a reddish-brown mixed-breed shepherd. Angel had no idea who this guy was. He walked over to the door, put his right hand on the knob, and as he turned the knob, he pulled his pistol out of his waist with his left hand. Angel opened the door and asked the man, "Do I know you?"

"Whoa, whoa…chill, man. Barry sent me. I just wanted to talk," replied the stranger.

"Barry and I are on bad terms. He is the competition. He has work, so why would he send you to me? And if he did send you to buy anything, he should have at least called me or given you my number. You didn't call me, and neither did Barry. You don't just pop up at my house. This is my home, *mi hogar*. I raise kids here. This is not a dope hole. For all I know, you can even be the police. You are here banging on my door like you lost your mind. What the hell are you on?"

Angel vividly remembers that the man looked like he was on some type of steroids and was on the verge of a rage. According to the toxicology report, he was on cocaine, crack, alcohol, and Xanax (alprazolam). The man began yelling, "Who do you think you are talking to, jit? You better respect me." The man was twenty-nine years old at the time, and there he was, calling Angel a jit, a little kid.

"Respect you? How about you respect me and my house and leave," Angel yelled back, stepping on the porch and closing the door behind him. The man's eyes looked beyond Angel with a non-comprehensive bewilderment, as if he couldn't understand the words coming out of Angel 's mouth.

After further rationalization, Angel realized that this man was high as a kite, so he just shook his head, shoved the gun back into his waistband, and said, "You know what? We just got off to a bad start. Let's try this again. My name is Angel . What's yours?" The man didn't answer but just kept the same look on his face and then started breathing a little harder.

Angel tried again. "Look, the insurance on this house doesn't cover dog bites, so can you please go back on the other side of the fence and I'll serve you whatever you want?"

The man still didn't respond. Angel put his left arm around the guy's back, his hand slightly resting on his shoulders. "Hey, come on, it isn't that serious. I will help you with whatever you want; I just want you to go on the other side of the fence so that my dogs won't accidentally bite you." The stranger responded by abruptly punching Angel on the left side of his jaw. Angel stumbled back about ten feet in shock while rubbing his jaw. "What the hell? I was just about to look out for you, and you HIT ME! On top of that, you hit like a bitch! You might as well leave, because I don't have anything for you now!" Angel exclaimed.

The stranger just stood there huffing and puffing. Angel reached in his back-left pocket and gripped his expandable ASP baton by its handle and demanded, "I said get off of my property!" Then he drew the ASP and swung it toward the floor, thus extending it to its full length of approximately two feet. At the tip of the ASP, there was a metal ball about the size of a marble.

At that precise moment, the stranger finally spoke. His provoking words were, "What exactly do you think you're going to do with that except piss me off?"

Amazed and enraged by this man's audacity, Angel rushed him. Keep in mind that Angel still had the pistol tucked in the front waistband of his shorts. If he wanted to shoot the man, he could have done it right then and there, but he didn't. He rushed the stranger and then actually swung the ASP at his head. The stranger raised his right arm, blocking the blow. Angel swung a second time, and again the stranger blocked the blow, inflicting the same impact on the upper-arm area. On the second connection, the ASP bent at the handle, giving it an arched look. Angel momentarily paused, looking at the ASP in amazement; he pondered how strong his assailant was.

At that moment the assailant grabbed Angel by the neck with both hands and pushed him back against the door. Angel threw the ASP on the floor. It had become useless. The assailant released his left hand from Angel's neck but still held on with his right hand. With his left hand free, the assailant then reached for the doorknob to the front door of Angel 's house.

Seeing an opening, Angel swung a right uppercut onto the assailant's left cheek bone and followed up with a left overhand hook that landed on the assailant's right eyebrow.

The assailant stumbled, bumping into and shoving a chair that was to the left of the front door. The assailant turned toward Angel and wrapped up with him, pushing him to the right side of the porch so that they ran into and shoved the other chair that was on the opposite side of the door and then ran into the chain-link fence.

Angel heard the assailant grumble, "Give me that gun."

The assailant went for the gun with his right hand. With rapid reflex, Angel grabbed his assailant's wrist with his left hand and squeezed for dear life. "What are you doing?" Angel asked. The assailant made a second attempt for the pistol with his left hand but stopped short because Angel caught his wrist in midair with his right hand. The assailant brought his restrained hands up to Angel 's chest in a struggle. Trying to break free, he pushed Angel into the fence and then threw his hands in the air, just like in "Y' in the the famous "YMCA" song. Angel threw a flurry of punches—six, to be exact. Right jab, left power, right jab, left power, all connecting beautifully, colliding with the man's eyes, eyebrows, and forehead area. Angel remembers the assailant's head bobbing back after each hit, but it wasn't enough. The assailant ducked his head down and threw himself onto Angel, wrapping his arms around him and pushing him into the corner of the fence. They both bounced off the fence the same way wrestlers or boxers bounce off the ropes in the ring. Angel pushed with all his strength, and they both stumbled, shoving themselves into a plastic lawn chair and sending it sliding back to the right of the door.

Angel pushed the assailant hard into the wall beside the front door. He got his arms wrapped under the assailant's underarms and, growling with all his might, tried to lift the man up and abruptly turn him away from the wall to take the assailant down, but to no avail. Angel failed, and instead they both stumbled back into the fence, only this time the assailant was the one cornered on the fence. The assailant, being the stronger of the two, pushed off the fence and power drove himself forward until they both stood in the center of the porch in front of the door. Then with a final strong shove, the assailant pushed Angel off himself.

Angel stumbled back about seven feet before regaining his balance. He was exhausted and realized how out of shape he was. He'd finally decided that enough was enough, and he reached for the pistol that should have been in his waistband. To his surprise, it was missing. In sudden horror, Angel 's eyes quickly darted over to the assailant's hands, and with some sort of relief, he realized that the pistol wasn't in either of his hands. Angel 's eyes quickly scanned the ground before him, and there, basking in the sun, lay the huge two-tone Smith & Wesson .40 caliber, gray nickel-plated on top, with a black bottom and handle.

Angel 's sight darted back to his assailant, and their eyes locked onto each other. The assailant then looked at the gun and returned his gaze, making eye contact once again with Angel . It all seemed to be in slow motion. The only thing Angel could hear was his own heart beating and heavy breathing. The assailant had a sadistic smirk on his face.

The gun was on the floor between them, closer to the assailant. Suddenly, the strange man went for it. Angel 's heart leaped in fear as he sprinted toward the assailant in football style with the palms of his hands pushing the assailant's shoulders upward and back, making him stumble backward. The assailant swung his arms wildly as he tried to regained his balance, and he ended up having to turn around, crashing into the disarranged lawn chair to the right of the door and clinging to the wall to hold himself up.

At that exact moment, Angel was recovering his pistol, momentarily taking his eyes off his assailant as he bent down to pick it up. Anticipating that his attacker would quickly recover and rush at him, Angel swung the pistol and his upper body up and squeezed the trigger. A loud blast came from the pistol along with the projectile that grazed the assailant's right cheekbone. They both stood in shock; Angel noticed a gash where the bullet had grazed the man. Incredibly the relentless assailant turned and picked up the green lawn chair closest to him. Angel let off another shot; this one slapped the man in the back. The assailant struggled but managed to pick up the chair, turned around growling, bent forward, and rushed Angel with the chair in front of him, looking like an infuriated bull. Angel, in fear of his life and being bulldozed into the ground, shot four more shots through the chair, thus bringing the assailant down and neutralizing the unlawful attacker. The green lawn chair fell at Angel 's feet. He flipped the chair out of his way and then brought both of his hands to his head in disbelief of what had just happened. "Look what you made me do to you! What's wrong with you? Are you crazy!?"

The afflicted man crawled backward, moaning in pain like an injured animal, and curled up into a fetal position next to the front door. Angel let his hands fall dead to his sides; he was exhausted and knew deep down inside that he would be going away for a long time. Maybe even for the rest of his life. His youngest son was only five months old; his oldest son was turning three in eighteen days. Everything he'd worked for, all his hustling and struggling, would be lost. "This can't be happening." His train of thought was abruptly disturbed by a screeching scream of horror that came from the lady next door. Then the front door cracked open half an inch. Junior had just recently learned how to stand on his tippy-toes and turn doorknobs.

Angel rushed to the front door before his son could pull the door open and was able to obstruct the toddler's view of the afflicted man.

He ran upstairs to his room. His wife, Anastasia, was there with the baby. She was leaning over him on the bed like a lioness protecting her cub. When he entered the room, he walked up to the bed, placed the toddler on the bed, and said, "I think I just killed a man."

She screamed, "No! Dammit! Why did you do that?"

Angel just stood there, still in shock, scared, and with a dumb expression on his face. Anastasia slapped him, trying to bring him back to reality. He said, "I don't know. I think he was trying to rob me or something. We started arguing. Then he hit me, we went to fighting and wrestling, one thing led to another, and I shot him down. He wouldn't stop, babe!" At this point Angel was afraid of criminal prosecution. He was ignorant of the law. He ran his hand through his hair, his mind racing, and he ran downstairs. Visions of the afflicted man rising like a zombie filled his mind with paranoia.

When Angel reached the front door, he saw his father-in-law, Stewie. stood there smoking a cigarette, analyzing the scene and the deceased man. Angel 's in-laws lived in the house next door. "What the hell happened, Angel ?" Stewie asked in his New Jersey accent.

"What the hell does it look like happened, Stewie? One second, we're arguing, the next we're fighting, and then this. The guy wouldn't stop. I think he was trying to rob me. He mentioned that Barry sent him. Barry and I are competitors, and we are on bad terms now, but I acted in self-defense! What do you think?"

"Eh, I don't know, Angel . I think the state of Florida has no self-defense. I know in New Jersey and New York, you would be all right, but I think here he has to have a weapon," Stewie informed Angel .

"Get out of here. Are you serious?" Angel rubbed his head in disbelief that this tragedy had taken place. "All right, listen, we are pressed for time. The cops will be here any minute. Help me get this stuff out of my house," Angel insisted.

They ran inside, and Angel grabbed some white garbage bags and began loading them with the dope and paraphernalia. They quickly filled two bags with more paraphernalia than dope. Then he grabbed his twelve gauge, and they rushed to the house next door to drop the stuff off in one of the rooms.

"Hey, Stewie, do you still have the gun I gave you?" Angel asked.

"Yeah, why?" Stewie responded.

"Let me get it," Angel demanded. "I am going to put it in the guy's hand."

"I think we should just leave it how it is."

"You said there is no self-defense in Florida unless he has a weapon, and I can't take that chance, Stewie. Give me the gun; I know what I'm doing!"

Stewie sighed and then went into a nearby closet, reached up to the upper shelf, and withdrew a gun pouch with a nine-millimeter Navy Arms pistol. All of Angel 's guns were stolen property, all purchased off the black market, so there was no way of tracing them back to him. They ran back next door. Angel was panicking, and in a frenzy of poor judgment, he wiped off the gun and placed it in the deceased man's hand, positioning the man's finger on the trigger. Feeling terrible about what he had just done, he was about to bend over and take the gun back, when suddenly, a police cruiser pulled up.

At this point Anastasia came out of the house with the kids and handed them to her father. Angel kissed and hugged them all. Hugging his wife last, he whispered in her ear with tears in his eyes, "I'm going away for a very long time."

Deep down inside he knew that if this had happened to a cop or a regular, legitimate professional man or business owner, that person would get self-defense, but not him, a poor young man of Hispanic descent with an extensive juvenile record, coming out of "el barrio de Hialeah." (Hialeah Neighborhood) He wouldn't even stand a chance against a prejudicial biased system or the local authorities or prosecutors. They're all a bunch of conviction-hungry hyenas.

No one could have anticipated or expected what was to come on that morning of mourning.

It started off as a regular Saturday morning. I was with my mother, whom we call Mima; my sister, Grace; and my youngest daughter, Maria Cristina, whose nickname is Nana. We were at the mall, shopping for a pair of shoes that would complement Maria's homecoming dress. Suddenly, my cell phone began to ring. It was Stewie, informing me that my son had just killed a man. The only thing that my mind registered now was life in prison or the electric chair. I began to cry and, I shouted, "NO! Oh no. Dios mio, no puede ser!" (God, this can't be!)

Stewie tried to calm me down by saying that it was in self-defense. "Calm down, caridad, it happened in his house, he acted in self-defense. He was protecting himself and his family."

But I continued to sob. I fell to my knees, crying and praying. Mima, Grace, and Maria were there for me along with plenty lot of curious shoppers who were wondering why I was on my knees crying in the middle of the mall.

I needed air. I had to get out of that place and away from all those people. I had to get to him, to his house, as soon as possible. We all went to the car, and I raced to drop everybody off at Grace's house. Then I raced to the scene. The block was closed off. There was a cluster of police cruisers and news crews. Yellow crime-scene tape and the mob of spectators made it impossible to drive up to my son's house or even close to the scene. I parked my car a block away and then rushed to his block. News crews and cameras were set up everywhere. I knew if I exposed the fact that the shooter was my son and that I needed to get through to his house, it would make the situation worse. I was able to get by the news crews and the spectators while remaining incognito. Step by step, I inched my way through the crowd, repeating "excuse me" as I journeyed through the crowd attentively listening to comments, criticism, and opinions. Finally, I reached the pricaridadbarrier of yellow crime-scene tape that sealed off the actual crime scene to avoid and prevent contamination.

There it stood before me, the house my son had moved to a year before. More spacious since they were having their second son.

The efficiency where they'd resided previously wasn't big enough, so they decided to rent the house for a year with an option to buy after. The building was big, with a rectangular-based structure. It had an orange-reddish ceramic tile roof. The pavement that mostly made up the front yard was painted to match the roof, and a chain-link fence surrounded the house. Hedges ran together alongside the fencing. At the foot of the hedges on either side of the house, there was a little garden of petite, colorful flowers, and the soil was covered in mulch. The pavement had white stone ornamental bricks in the shape of miniature hills that bordered the edges of the little garden. Each little garden was approximately three feet wide. At the front of the house, three big rectangular windows went left to right across the second floor—a window for each bedroom. On the bottom, the ground floor, were larger rectangular windows. Toward the center of the house, there was a regular-sized window that belonged to the living room, and beneath it was a bigger garden about three feet wide and fifteen feet long that was an exact replica of the other two little gardens. The only differences were the miniature palm-tree type of plant that stood about three feet tall at the center of the larger garden and the fountain with two cherubs pouring water out of small buckets at the right. At the end of the fountain toward the bottom right side of the house was a front porch that had a white door and overhang of cement with a margin tile roof. The overhang was attached to the wall of the house right beneath the third window of the second floor. The overhang was approximately five feet wide and about seven to eight feet long and covered the entire porch. The two green heavy-duty plastic lawn chairs that normally sat on the porch to either side of the front door were disarranged as if a struggle had taken place. And I couldn't help but notice that one of the lawn chairs had bullet holes going through it. The golden-brown and black welcome mat that normally lay at the foot of the door was submerged in a puddle of blood that came from the deceased man who lay beside it. He wore red-and-white Jordan sneakers, blue jeans, and a tank top. He had a beard like Fidel Castro and a low haircut.

Instantly, a vision flashed in my mind that it could've

been Angel, my only son, lying there in a pool of his own blood instead of this other man. At that moment, it hit me. I felt like a wrecking ball had hit me in the chest, as if some unseen force had just ripped my heart right out of my body, and I was gripped with horror. The pain hurt so much that I had to grab my chest. I prayed and thanked God that it wasn't my baby. I heard an agonizing cry coming from a woman sitting on a nearby bench. From her sobs, I knew right away, without a doubt in my mind, that it was her baby lying on the porch in that pool of blood. As a woman and mother, I was filled with deep sorrow, and my heart went out to her. I was crying and genuinely wanted to run up to her, give her a hug, cry with her, and apologize to her, but I held back in fear of her reaction. I heard one spectator tell another, "That's what they get for living that life, involved in that drug business. One is dead, and the other's going to jail."

CHAPTER 4

Different Scenarios

What really took place on that morning of mourning? Besides God, only Angel and the deceased man really know. There weren't any actual witnesses to the incident. There were only "witnesses" who came after the fact. There were ludicrous versions being said of what happened that morning. Some accounts were even ridiculous.

The state prosecutors made up their own theory of what they believed happened that day. They believed the deceased man was the victim and he only went to Angel's house that morning to purchase narcotics. Angel got infuriated because the man hadn't called first, thus breaking one of Angel's rules. Angel, being the "evil villain," without further provocation, shot the man right on the porch of his own home in broad daylight. The stranger—whose name was Manny—tried to escape by jumping the fence, and Angel shot him in the back, then continued to mercilessly shoot him executioner style while the victim pitifully tried to shelter himself from the raining bullets under the green plastic lawn chair. Finally, Angel staged the scene by placing a pistol in Manny's hand and bending the ASP to make himself look innocent. They said an altercation never took place since Angel had no injuries except for a "scratch on the left side of his neck and nick on his knuckles," and the bruises on the victim's face, eyebrow, forehead, and eye area were caused by chips of the green plastic chair.

Another version told by people on the streets was that Angel's wife, Anastasia, shot Manny out of fear while Angel and Manny were wrestling. Then, worried that his beloved wife would go to prison for life, Angel grabbed the gun and proceeded to shoot Manny, finishing him off and thus taking the blame.

Well, what if it had gone the other way around? What if this went deeper than what it really seemed? Manny had stated that Barry sent him. Now let's place the pieces of this puzzle together. When Barry was questioned during depositions, he admitted that he was hanging out with Manny on September 23, which was the Friday night prior to the morning of mourning. They were friends and were partying in a group of about five men. They went to strip clubs, getting trashed and highly intoxicated. When the men were done club hopping, they all went back to Barry's house, which was on Fourteenth Street in between East Third and Fourth Avenues. They were on Angel 's block since he lived on Thirteenth Street in between East Third and Fourth.

Barry admitted that Manny was agitated and that they even had an argument. Barry stated that he told Manny not to go to Angel 's house. He also admitted that Manny did not know Angel . Barry said that Manny left his residence angry and he assumed Manny was on his way to his own home on Fifteenth Street. Now ask yourself this: How would Angel know that Barry sent this man, unless the man told Angel this for a fact? Why didn't Barry call Angel to warn him that an infuriated, highly intoxicated man might be on the way to his house? Barry knows what he did that day. He got that poor man trashed, sold him a dream, and then sent him on a crash-dummy mission. Finally, Barry covered his tracks and washed his hands of it.

Angel mentioned how he and Barry were "competition" and on "bad terms." Prior to this whole situation, Barry, Manny, and the rest of their "gang" disliked the fact that my son had moved into their neighborhood. This was a bunch of grown-ass men in their thirties still living at home with their parents. They just couldn't stand to see a twenty-year-old young man moving into what they thought was their block, making moves and making money, living comfortably in this city. They envied Angel and hated on him even though he was of their own kind. Angel and Barry were on bad terms because Barry was whining and complaining to Angel that he couldn't make money ever since Angel moved into the block. Angel explained to Barry that business is business and that the city of Hialeah is big enough for anyone who wants to hustle and make money.

Their arguing ended up in multiple threats toward one another. They had established an understanding that neither of them would back down. Barry and his goons underestimated Angel . They mistook his kindness for weakness. They believed that because he was only twenty years old, he was dumb, young, and inexperienced. They were right to a certain extent, but Momma didn't raise no fool either. Their plan was to lure Angel outside of his home and land a solid sucker punch to knock him out. Then they would disarm Angel and rob him or do God knows what to take him out of commission. The problem is that "you can plan a pretty picnic, but you can't always predict the weather." Maybe everyone would've been happier if it would have ended the other way around, with Angel getting shot and killed by his own pistol right there in front of his own home. With no witnesses at all, Manny could've run and gotten away clean. The authorities would have ruled it gang or drug related, and it would have been just another unsolved murder case, swept under the rug, or a cold case like the ones they show on the tips hotline shows.

Or the defendant could've entered the dwelling, shutting the door behind him, leaving Angel laid out on his own front porch bleeding to death while his defenseless wife and kids were inside completely vulnerable. Maybe he would have just taken what he could find and left. Maybe he would have hurt the kids or Anastasia while trying to squeeze information out of her regarding a secret stash of dope or money. Who knows? Only God knows. Regardless, in Angel 's case it was a lose-lose situation either way. Damned if he did, damned if he didn't.

Now it's easier to speak from the sidelines about what you would have done differently, somewhat like a football fan watching the game from the comfort of his couch, seeing things from the outside looking in, usually criticizing the quarterback and saying things like "Aw, come on, man!" and "I would have done this" or "I would have done that. I would have thrown it to him!" But on that field in the spur of the moment, under that intense adrenaline rush of overgrown, barbaric defensive linemen blitzing full speed at the fan in a game of "kill the man with the ball," odds are the average man would fall under pressure because he is just that: average. An average man who is not trained professionally and is not put into those types of predicaments on a regular basis would panic, run, and yell like a maniac, and nine times out of ten, he would fumble before the point of impact, get sacked, or throw an interception. Thus, what appeared easy or simple from the sidelines is really an underrated and extremely difficult predicament that the majority of people would never have to face. God forbid you ever do, because you never know how you might react to a spontaneous situation such as the one Angel was confronted with.

CHAPTER 5

Taken into Custody

As the police arrived on the scene, Angel took hold of his wife on her parents' driveway next door. He hugged her and softly whispered in her ear, "Hug me, baby. I'm probably going to jail for a long time."

As they stood there embracing and crying in each other's arms, the remorse that Angel felt was overwhelming. He had just killed a man, and no matter how justified you may be, if you have any human morals left in you, it's only normal to feel remorse and guilt after taking a life.

It weighed on him so much that his legs could no longer hold him up, so he suddenly sat down. Anastasia crouched down with him, still hugging him. They were oblivious to the fact that the police officers had come up on them with their pistols drawn and aimed at Angel . Anastasia defensively raised her right hand, facing the officer and yelling,, "stop! Don't shoot! Don't hurt him, please!"

The female officer screamed, "Where's the gun?"

"It's on the couch. I shot him in self-defense. He was trying to rob me," Angel responded.

"Put your hands behind your back!" yelled the female officer. Angel complied.

She handcuffed him, and then she asked, "Where's the guy you shot?"

"He is next door on my front porch," Angel replied. The female officer signaled to her comrades to go to the house next door. She then helped Angel up and placed him against the police cruiser. Angel instructed Anastasia to take his wallet and cell phone out of his pockets. The officer then placed Angel in the back seat of the cruiser. His wife stood by the open window of the police car door and said, "Everything's going to be all right, baby. Just calm down," as she tried to sooth and comfort her husband.

He snapped back, "No, it's not, Anastasia. You don't know how these cops work. All they want to do is lock men up!"

"But you were protecting me and the kids and yourself in your home," she said, breaking into a cry at the thought of the word *home*.

"They don't care, and that's not how they're going to see it!" Angel answered his wife.

Just then two officers who had just arrived on the scene walked about three feet behind Anastasia, bent over to look through the cruiser window, and broke into laughter. Officer Number One: "Hey, what do we have here?"

Officer Number Two: "Hey, don't I know you?"

"No, you don't know me." Angel fired back.

Officer Number Two: "Looks like we got you now!"

Officer Number One whistled.

"I didn't do anything, I was protecting myself in my home!" Angel yelled at the cops and then looked toward Anastasia. "Do you see what I mean babe?"

At that precise moment, Officer Number Two demanded, "Excuse me, miss, we're going to need you to step away from the car at this time."

With tears in her eyes, Anastasia kept eye contact with Angel as if waiting for his approval. He nodded for her to go inside, but she stayed. Angel glared at the two cops as they stepped closer to Anastasia. Officer Number Two exclaimed, "Excuse me, ma'am, PLEASE STEP AWAY FROM THE CAR!"

Before the officer could even place a hand on her, Angel 's father-in-law, Stewie, intervened, exclaiming, "Hey, that's my daughter! What seems to be the problem, Officer?"

All of a sudden, the cop changed his whole attitude from corrupted jerk to Robo Cop. Officer Number Two cleared his throat. "Sir, we need for your daughter to step away from the vehicle."

Stewie gently put his hands on his daughter's shoulders and rubbed up and down as if to warm her. "Come on, honey, let's go." As Stewie and Anastasia backed away from the car, a detective walked up to them and began talking to them. The other two officers who were harassing them glared one last time at Angel and walked away. The detective and Stewie spoke back and forth in an audible tone. After a couple nods of understanding, they all walked to an unmarked sedan. Stewie helped Anastasia into the back seat of the car. Eventually Angel, Anastasia, her parents, Stewie's mother, and all three kids were escorted to the Hialeah police station and taken into custody for questioning.

They were segregated from each other. The detectives interrogated Anastasia and her parents first. One thing led to another, and Anastasia's parents signed a consent form giving consent for the police to search their house and get the shotgun and drugs. They told the detectives that it all belonged to Angel and that they wanted it out of their house. Sure enough, the police retrieved the drugs and shotgun.

Meanwhile, Angel was handcuffed in another room, wondering what was taking so long. He eventually fell asleep. Approximately twelve hours later, the detectives decided to interrogate Angel . They asked him if he was hungry or thirsty. Common sense would have told you he was, but he said he wasn't. instead he went off to use the bathroom. The detective asked Angel if he was interested in a cigarette, but Angel refused.

The two detectives were both male. One was named Aaron, and the other was named Morales. Aaron had a mustache, light eyes, and brown hair that was excessively dyed to hide the gray. His mustache was also overly dyed the same color as well. He was wearing a long-sleeved yellow dress shirt with some tie and dark slacks. Morales was bald and had on a collared uniform shirt, the type that only has three neck buttons and a badge stitched to the left side of the shirt on his chest. The shirt was beige, and he wore blue jeans.

Before they asked Angel, what happened, they explained how it worked: "What we do, Angel, is we gather all the information together, and if all the stories match, then we can conclude what might have happened. If the stories don't match up, then we have a problem. We then begin to use our skills to pick at and put together what we believe happened. This is so you have an idea of what's going on, but before we begin, let me read you your Miranda rights; then Morales will need you to initial and sign some papers, okay?" Detective Aaron stated.

"Okay," Angel replied.

The detective read Angel his Miranda rights, took samples of his DNA, and had him initial and sign some documents. After all the "politically correct" mumbo jumbo, Detective Aaron asked Angel what happened. Detective Aaron had a legal pad and was writing and going over things he had already written down. He then turned on a digital hand-held recorder, and Angel began speaking.

"Well, I made breakfast for my wife, myself, and the kids. Junior and I, my oldest son, were about to go watch a movie, when suddenly, I heard my dog barking hysterically. I walked to my window and saw an intruder walking toward my door. He banged on my door. I opened the door and realized I didn't know who this guy was. I thought he was lost. I asked him to step back onto the other side of the fence because I didn't want him to get bit by one of my dogs. The strange intruder seemed highly intoxicated and agitated. He wasn't listening to my request, so I asked him to leave. Then we began to argue, and suddenly, he punched me on my jaw. I extended my expandable ASP and hit him with it in the arm. The intruder went for his waist, drawing a firearm, so I went for my gun and shot him down."

The detectives stared Angel down coldly.

Detective Aaron asked, "Is there anything else you want to say?"

"No, that's it. That's what happened." Angel responded.

Aaron said, "Okay, are you sure this is all you want the state to hear?"

"Yeah, sure, that's it. Can me and my family go home now?"

"Well, there seems to be a problem, Angel . Unfortunately, the stories didn't match.

"Why? What did they say?" Angel asked.

"I can't tell you what they said. All I can tell you is that the stories didn't match," Detective Aaron replied.

Angel thought to himself, this is one of their tricks.

Detective Aaron continued, "For example, have you ever tried to fix something that wasn't broken and ended up breaking it, but it could still be fixed? Or do you know anything about the drugs and shotgun found at your in-law's house?"

Wow. Just then Angel felt as if an electric current had gone through his body. Something had gone wrong. Detective Aaron was talking about the gun placed in Manny's hand and the drugs and shotgun next door. But how did he know? It took less than a minute for Angel to figure this one out. Like a tribe of lions, or better yet, a pack of hyenas, they attacked the weakling out of the group of prey. The detectives went after Anastasia and her parents. First, they slammed handcuffs on the table, then threatened not only to lock them up but to put the kids in Department of Children and Family (DCF). That's how they got them to fully cooperate. Since Anastasia and her parents had never been through anything like this, they folded under pressure. Angel remained silent with a dumbfounded look on his face. He thought hard about what his next move would be.

Detective Aaron impatiently smirked at Angel 's facial expression. He looked to the side and then exploded out of his chair, slamming the pad down on the table with one hand, and began to jab his other hand, pointing his index finger in Angel 's face and chest. He was leaning over the table and exclaimed, "I'm through playing games with you! Let's get something straight in here. I've been doing this a long time. I looked you up, and you are a signal 150 career criminal since the age of *fourteen years old*! I know what you are, and I know what you do. It's been a very long day and night. You think I don't know what's going on? You want to play games? I can play games, but as of right now, I can charge your in-laws with racketeering and your wife with racketeering accessory to the murder. I can have all the children placed in DCF custody. You think I don't have the power to do that? Just try me. Call my bluff, I dare you. How old is that baby out there, huh? A couple of months? Well, he needs his mommy right now, don't you agree? Well, picture him in the arms of a woman he doesn't know. Think of the trauma that'll be caused to all the kids when they're stripped from all of you and separated from each other." The scenario was vividly playing in Angel 's mind. He could see a picture of the kids screaming, crying, and fighting as they were forced away. "Better yet," continued Detective Aaron, "think about your pretty little wife and mother-in-law going to jail. How long do you think they'll be there before some gorilla-looking dyke makes them their bitch?"

Just then Detective Morales stood up and put his arm in front of Detective Aaron as if to hold him back. They made eye contact, and Detective Aaron stood up straight, adjusted his tie, and sat back down. Detective Morales slid a paper showing the signed consent from Angel 's in-laws to search their house. He said in a low tone, "They threw you under the bus, kid," and then he sat back down.

Angel stared at the paper with tears streaming down his face. He didn't care about the paper or that they threw him under the bus because it was previously agreed that he would take the fall to spare them. What tore him apart were the vivid images of Detective Aaron threatening his family. Through clenched teeth Angel asked, "Why are you doing this?"

Detective Aaron answered, "Somebody lost their life today because of you. It's your fault. You are definitely going to jail tonight. The question is, are you going to be a man about it and admit your faults or a coward and drag your family down with you?"

At that precise moment, Angel had a flashback of a night he, his wife, and her parents spent together hanging out, enjoying some drinks. Stewie, Angel, and Anastasia were all high. Stellar, Anastasia's mom, had only been drinking. They were discussing the consequences of his business. Not to ruin the moment, Angel calmed down their concerns by saying, "You guys have nothing to worry about. I'll be in and out the game before anything bad happens. I'll invest in something, and if the shit ever hits the fan, I will take full responsibility and say you guys didn't know anything."

Angel looked up at the detectives with a stone-cold face. "What do you want from me?" he asked.

The detectives looked at each other, and Aaron said, "I have questions prepared on this legal pad that I'm going to ask you. Just tell us what we want to hear."

Angel chuckled as if he couldn't believe his ears and shook his head. "I'll say what you want to hear, and I'll answer your questions, but how will I know for sure that you'll let my family go?"

"Well, Angel, truth is you won't really know for sure, but if you tell us what we want to hear like you're saying, and it sounds good and convincing, then, for what it's worth I give you my word, your family goes home tonight. I promise."

Morales looked at Aaron and nodded his head, then he looked back at Angel . "I second that notion, Angel . You have my word as well."

"There, you see, you have our word either way. If you clearly state yourself on the recording that they did nothing wrong, I don't see how we can keep them here—right, Morales?" Aaron stated, turning to Morales as he asked his partner for assurance.

"Nope. We can't keep them if you exonerate them, Angel," declared Detective Morales.

Angel nodded his head, understanding what he had to do. They went through the motions of restarting the digital hand-held recorder, reading him his Miranda rights and everything all over again. They stopped the first session, which lasted an entire hour of recording, and labeled it "the per-interrogation." Only Angel and the detectives knew what happened during that hour, and now, so do you. The proof lies within the truth, but the fact of the matter is that on that night, the whole family was released as part of the deal.

Angel confessed and told them what really happened as previously discussed earlier on the morning of mourning. He admitted to placing the gun in the deceased man's hand, and he answered all the detectives' questions. Whenever he answered a question and it wasn't what the detectives wanted to hear, they would ask again or rephrase the question as a hint to let him know that he was messing up. He confessed that the drugs and shotgun were his and that his family was innocent, stating that they only did what he made them do or pressured them to do. What gave him the strength to continue incriminating himself was his big heart. He loved his friends so much that he considered them family. He even tried vigorously to merge that little family into his own blood family. His adoration for the children, his wife, his little brothers-in-law, his mother- and father-in-law, and even his two grandmothers-in-law was immense. He stood by them through thick and thin, for better or for worse, and held their heads above water through some of their toughest times.

It was time to Go to Miami Dade County Jail. He was charge with second degree murder.

John 15:13 says, "Greater love hath no man than this, that a man lay down his life for his friends." Unfortunately, not even a year after his incarceration, Anastasia broke Angel 's heart to pieces. They all abandoned him and left him for dead. Left him alone in his sickness, his addiction, and his insanity. The details will be explained in future chapters, but for right now, they simply couldn't understand or comprehend his pain. They broke like water and leaked away. But real blood is thicker than water, and thank God Angel has a real family. A big family that loves, adores, and supports him always.

CHAPTER 6

What I Left Behind

My family has always stuck together; we believe there's power in unity. Imagine moving to a foreign land where not many people speak your language and vice versa; to have to start from scratch; to establish, from the bottom up, the foundation of a struggling family that would either prosper or perish. Well, that's what my family did when we left Cuba and migrated to the United States, the wonderful land of opportunity! We had no choice. I was born during the years that Fidel Castro and his revolutionaries took over.

My family owned a farm in the city of Matanzas. with many acres of land and all sorts of farm animals, and a variety of fruits, vegetables, and sugarcane grew in our land. My grandpa and father were known for breeding the best gamecocks, which were also known as fighting roosters and in Spanish were referred to as *gallos finos*. We were country folk, and we were happy.

Eventually the unexpected happened. Castro began confiscating land and animals and turning them into state property. If anyone resisted, they would be arrested as a political prisoner for going against the revolutionary movement. In some cases, they would even be shot to death. Castro and his goons were and still are a force to be reckoned with today. They had taken over the whole country, and there was little my dad, grandpa, and uncles could do. If they'd attempted to fight fire with fire, the results would've been devastating to my family. In Spanish we have a saying that goes, "Vista larga, pasos cortos." It means you must take short steps while keeping a long-range vision, or in other words, you must think outside the box and have a futuristic state of mind. "Humility defeats pride; pride defeats man. My grandparents had to be wise. "Vista larga, pasos cortos." Our family's future depended on it.

So, my grandparents sent their two oldest daughters, Tia Congo and Tia Ofelia, with their husbands and my cousin Oscar, who was Tia Congo's son, as scouts into the city of Miami in the state of Florida. Eventually they found jobs and housing and saw that Florida offered the chance of a better future, so they requested that the whole family move to the United States. I was six years old when my family put in for the change of venue. My grandparents forfeited our citizenship in Cuba and requested that we be allowed to move to the United States. At first the Cuban government was reluctant, but eventually it approved. Once the request was approved, the government explained the circumstances. There would be two armed inspectors on motorcycles with padlocks. When the inspectors arrived at the property, the whole family would have to exit the residence with only two bags per person. The two bags could only contain the personal belongings that we would be taking with us to the United States. The entire family would then be escorted off the property. The door would be padlocked, and the home would then become property of the state.

We waited, and every morning my grandma would sit on the porch, listening for the loud sound of the motorcycle engines and exhaust coming from a far. We thought the government had lied to us and tricked us. I was already twelve years old. We had been waiting for six years with our bags packed. It seemed as if we would never get to go to the land of opportunity. Not to mention that we were running out of time because my mother was pregnant and expecting a baby. If she gave birth before we left, we would have to start the process all over again in order to include the newborn child.

Then, the morning of May 7, 1971, the miracle happened! We were all awake. My dad and grandpa were out working in the fields. I was outside on the porch with my grandma. My mom, eight months pregnant by now with my little sister, was inside with my siblings. Suddenly, my grandma heard it, a peculiar buzzing far off in the distance. She cupped her ear with her hand as if straining for assurance and then turned to me and said, "Maria, go tell your father, grandpa, and uncle Pepe that the inspectors are on their way. Hurry!" She didn't say this in english either.

My heart leaped inside my chest. "This is it!" I thought to myself. I hopped off the porch and ran through the field as fast as my legs could carry me. I found them, each with a garden hoe in his hands used for weeding and tilling. I yelled, "Pipo, Abuelo, ya vienen los inspectores!" (Dad, Grandpa, the inspectors are coming!) Their eyes were wide open, looking at each other with a shocked expression of utter disbelief. I had to yell again, "Dale, dale! Apurencen, vamos!" (Let's go, let's go! Hurry come on!) They dropped their farm tools and sprinted with me back through the fields toward the house.

Back at the house, we could hear the faraway buzzing of the motorcycles piercing through the quiet country air. Our neighbors who lived about an acre away came rushing over to our home. They must have heard the buzzing as well. My best friend, Xiomara, was there. My mom, grandma, auntie, and my uncle's father's grandpa were all shuffling around the house making last-minute preparations. My younger sister, Victoria, and I were giving away things like our mattresses and small furniture out of the back door. Then I embraced my best friend along with my pet hen named Pita. I gave Pita to Xiomara, and she said she would take good care of her for me. We were crying. As a matter of fact, the whole family was crying.

Finally, when the inspectors pulled up on the property, we were already waiting outside with our bags. They made sure we only had two bags each. They searched our Jeep and then padlocked our home, taping a paper on the door that read, "Propiedad Del Estado" (Property of the State). We loaded up on the Jeep and took one last look through teary eyes at our home, our animals, and our farm. Off to the side stood our neighbors whom we had grown to love as family, embracing each other, crying, and waving good-bye to us. We waved good-bye back. Xiomara yelled, "Cuidare a Pita y a todos los animalitos. Estan en buenas manos!" (I'll take care of Pita and the rest of the animals. They're in good hands!)

I yelled back, "Gracias. Te amo, mi amiga. Nunca te olvidare!" (Thank you. I love you, my friend. I'll never forget you!)

The Jeep's motor roared as it came to life, and we took off. We all cried and held each other, staring back as the view of the house shrank away in the distance. That night the government provided us with a hotel room to spend the night. The following morning, we boarded the plane. It took off, and that was my last view of my country. I got to watch from the small window of the plane as my beautiful island shrank in the distance.

Then, we landed on US soil. It was 1971. My two aunties (the scouts), their husbands, and my cousins Oscar and Ileana waited for us at the airport. When we arrived at the airport, they greeted and accepted us. "Plantamos banderas." (We've planted our flag.)

Everyone who was willing and able had to work. We started doing what we knew best, farming. Even I had to work. I got a job picking tomatoes and other types of fruits. My pay was just a nickel per basket, and it was hard work and very difficult for a young girl to carry those heavy baskets around. The Mexicans had a system that was very effective. They worked in teams. They had pickers who would pick up and pile all the fruit off to the side and carriers who would load the piles of food into their baskets and haul them off to the trucks. They would then hand the basket to the man loading the truck in exchange for a nickel or five pennies and a new empty basket. The Mexicans would share their earnings and distribute them among each other. I found it very rewarding to tuck my dirty-blond hair into my hat and blend in as a carrier instead of doing all the work by myself.

As I got older, I got better jobs working in supermarkets. I learned the English language very well at school to get better jobs working at the supermarket. I learned that when some of the food was approaching its expiration date, a lot of it was discarded. I couldn't believe my eyes; perfectly good food being thrown away in the garbage. On some occasions, they donated it to charity or churches, but for the most part, into the dumpster it went. Well, not if I could help it, and not as long as I had little siblings. My family's needs would be met by any means necessary.

"Hey, caridad! When you get a chance, I need you to toss the expiring food out back, okay?" the supermarket manager would say.

"Okay, no problem, sir," I would reply. I would then go out back with all types of goodies. Gallons of milk, eggs, bread, and so on. I'd stack everything in boxes, disguise it, and hide it behind the dumpster. At the end of my shift, I would wait until the coast was clear and then load up my Camaro. This would literally put food on our table.

My father, "Pipo," got a job working as a security guard. We were all US residents, but shortly after landing in the United States, my mother, "Mima," gave birth to the first US citizen of our family. Once my baby sister, Grace, was old enough to be taken to daycare, Mima started working in factories. My grandma, Abuela, was a gambler. From Cuba to the States, she was a hustler, she bet on wrestling and cockfights and was a good old-fashioned tomboy, a tough country girl, a brawler. She was even known to duke it out with men. Abuela had a very hoarse voice and almost sounded like a man.

My father's side of the family was dark skinned and Indian mixed with Congo, African. My mom is white as snow with pink features. Her whole side of the family is vampire white. Till this day, the sun hurts her skin. She must wear sunblock and long-sleeve shirts and carry an umbrella on hot, sunny days. The mixture gave me and my siblings a beautiful skin complexion of a white, sun-kissed tan.

My grandfather, Abuelo, was a hardworking farmer. He even made it to the newspaper. The reporters were commending him for being seventy-six years old and still working so hard. The photographers took pictures of him holding up a sweet potato. We were all so proud to see it! Our family is a breed of hardworking hustlers with brains and muscle. We are thoroughbred go-getters by any means necessary.

We were survivors.

Every Christmas Eve (known as Noche Buena in the Spanish culture), New Year's Eve, and on birthdays, we would get together as a family. Especially on Christmas Eve, when all the men would get together and roast a whole pig, drink beer, and watch the children play outside, while the women were inside cooking the side dishes and desserts. The side dishes consisted of *arroz congree* (a mixture of white rice and black beans), *yuca* (a beet-like root vegetable), *ensaladas* (salads), and *platanitos maduros* (deep-fried ripe plantains) or *tostones* (deep-fried flattened green plantains). For dessert there would be marshmallow fruit cocktails, flan (sweetened custard with caramel topping), and *turron* (nougat made from almonds and honey). These were all samples of Spanish cuisine. These festivities were instilled in us as traditions that we would pass on to the next generation and future generations to come.

Abuela was the first to die and be buried in US soil. She had a massive heart attack while watching a wrestling match. She was a wrestling fanatic! She would throw fits and curse out the opposing wrestler, especially if he beat her favorite wrestler. Her reactions were always very comical to us until she had the massive heart attack and died. Abuela was the heart of our family. We mourned and cried. We felt alone. There was a void in all of us that we couldn't fill.

The next day I asked Abuelo, "Y ahora que, Abuelo? Que vamos ha hacer ahora?" (Now what, Grandpa? What are we going to do now?) I was scared; I felt lost, and the future seemed uncertain.

After some contemplation, he answered in Spanish, "We will continue to do what she wants from us. We will continue to survive. We are farmers. Your grandmother and I planted our little seeds, and with a lot of protection and affection, we raised our plants until they grew fruit, and one day if God wants those fruits to bear more fruit, the circle of life will continue, and our legend will live forever inside their souls. Everyone must die one day. That is inevitable. One day you and your little sisters and your little brother will get married, have a home, and have children, either little girls or little boys, but always remember everything we have taught you. In unity there is power, honor, and loyalty. The world is full of vipers, rats, fleas, ticks, and snakes full of treason and wickedness. United you can overcome any tribulation, but individually you'll always be eaten alive. Never let fortune or fame separate you. Always united, always strong. A family always united and always strong is a family moving forward. Long view, short steps. I've lost the love of my life momentarily in this world, but soon I will be with her. Likewise, one day we will all be together in God's paradise."

Tia Lea's husband, Pepe, was the second person in our family to pass away and be buried in US soil. I can't quite remember exactly what he died from. I just remember he was very ill. My best bet would be that it was his liver because he was a drunk. One time he got so drunk that he crashed into a fence while driving his Jeep. Somehow, he flew out of the Jeep into the fence. No biggie. He stumbled back into the Jeep, and by the grace of God made it home without crashing again or hurting anyone. When he got home, everyone noticed blood coming down the side of his head and all over his shirt and pants. After a closer examination, Tia Lea realized that Pepe's ear was missing. It was completely gone. Pepe said he could hear just fine. The women were in shock and horrified. On the other hand, Pipo and Abuelo found some humor in it. We traced back to the scene of the accident and found Pepe's ear hanging on the fence. Pipo and Abuelo took turns speaking into the ear. "Oye, Pepe, tu me copias? Copiando! Copiando! Pepe, responde inmediatamente!" (Hey, Pepe, do you copy? Over! Over! Do you read me? Pepe respond immediately!) They all laughed, but then they hurried to the hospital where Pepe got his ear sewn back onto his head.

We will always love and miss our loved ones who have passed. Abuela, Pepe, Abuelo, Tia Lea, Tia Congo, and Pipo. The deaths after Pepe didn't come until years later, though, after my mom and dad got separated. Pipo was cheating on Mima with a woman named Myra, and he got her pregnant with my youngest and only half-sister, Molly. Molly grew up participating in our gatherings and parties as part of the family.

Eventually I fell in love, got married, and had my first child, a baby girl named Julie. Then my sister Victoria got married and had her first child, Rudolf, followed by her second son, Aries. I got divorced, remarried, and became pregnant again, but I decided to have an abortion. After that came my first and only son, Angel, followed by my last child and youngest daughter, Maria Cristina. My second-youngest sister, Grace, got married at sixteen years old and had her first child, whom she named Melissa. Around the same time, my cousin Omar got married and had his first little girl. My brother, Valdito, also got married and had his first child, Andy. Grace had her second child, Johnny, and Valdito and his wife had their second child, Christian. Then Molly had five children of her own. Our family grew and expanded. The new seeds had been planted for the next generation. As the kids got older, we continued the traditional get-togethers and threw parties just like always on Noche Buena, New Year's Eve, and birthdays, trying to instill unity and our traditions into their little minds. They all bonded together and usually had a blast. We tried to make history repeat itself by celebrating our family's traditions.

CHAPTER 7

That Child of Mine

At first Angel was a wonderful baby boy, cute as could be. He was always smiling and ate all his food. And he was a tough little rug rat! I used to horseplay with him. I'd throw him on the bed and then throw my whole body on top of him. It was so funny. I could hear him grunting as he pushed up, and when I would get off of him, he would laugh. Each time I'd do it, he'd just laugh uncontrollably. He was an incredible kid. I knew then that he could withstand the pressures of the world. He shoplifted for the first time at four years old. I couldn't believe it. He turned into a little menace. He loved Michael Jackson. One time, while we were watching Michael Jackson's music video "I'm Bad," the chorus kicked in, and Angel jumped off the couch, trying to mimic Michael's dance moves.

Angel's father went to federal prison when my son turned six years old. Before his incarceration, he introduced me to cocaine and heavy drinking. He was an abusive, violent man. We used to get into fistfights, and he even hit me while I was pregnant with Angel . He was always cheating on me and was in and out of jail. He was never there for Angel or Maria Cristina. He ended up doing ten years in prison, day for day. So, there I was, all alone, an alcoholic and cocaine addict with the responsibility of raising three kids by myself. I'd never raised a boy before, so I figured I had to be tough on Angel in order for him to grow up into a straight-shooting, successful man. My biggest fear was for him to become some hoodlum gangster or bad man.

I got sick and tired of being sick and tired. The drinking and substance abuse turned me into the type of person I didn't want to be. I could not continue on that path any longer. One night I was awake in the middle of the night, drinking as usual, when I once again asked God for help. The TV was turned on, although I wasn't watching it or even looking at the screen, when I heard a commercial asking, "Do you need help?" and saying if so, to call the number on the screen. I raised my head in response, found a pen, wrote down the number, and then made that phone call. I reached out for help and entered a program of recovery on October 6, 1993. I finished four months of rehab and continued with support from a twelve-step program. I got a sponsor, worked the steps, and did service. I also got close to God once again. You see, I believe God never left me. I was the one who did not want anything to do with God or any type of spiritual life. I went back to church and became a member. I was beginning to feel better about myself.

However, I confess that in my addiction and insanity, I overreacted toward my children, verbally and physically abusing them. Sometimes, I would lose control and beat my son, screaming at him at the top of my lungs. On more than one occasion, my sister Grace, my mom, or my daughters would have to pull me off of him. I would use my sandals or twigs from the backyard.

This kid was something else, though.

I put him in the Children's Psychiatric Center (CPC) and boxing to see if that would release some of his extra energy. CPC diagnosed him with hyperactive disorder and attention deficit disorder (ADD). They prescribed him Ritalin. His grades were outstanding, but he was always fighting in school and getting suspended, and he even called his teacher the *B* word. He began stealing book bags at nine years old, and by the time he was ten, he was stealing bikes. He was incorrigible. No matter how many times I kicked his butt, he would just shake it off. I remember one time while I was whooping him, he started laughing. Literally laughing uncontrollably. I yelled to my mother, "Mira, Mima—esta poseido con demonios!" (Look, Mima—he's possessed by demons!) Mima shook her head from side to side and began laughing. I was furious and exasperated, but I couldn't help but laugh at the end too.

Overall, though, Angel was a lovable kid, always hugging and kissing everybody. He would give me, Mima, Grace, and Victoria back massages when we were tense. He was full of charisma. A real Casanova and naturally a smooth operator. My sister Grace used to always sing to him, saying, "You can't always get what you want!" Over and over she would tease and taunt him. Eventually, he would find a way to manipulate her into the palm of his little hand. He would always get his way. Even with Grace's little song, he would still always find a way to get on her last nerve, until she would yell and yank him by the ear.

As time went by, he grew older, and it isn't easy growing up in poverty. I always tried to provide and give him what I could, but he was his own man. He wanted to make his own money, be the man of the house, help bring food to the table, and make ends meet. As he grew and got older, I couldn't beat him like before. He wouldn't let me. He was bigger and stronger now. He got exceptionally good at blocking and ducking and dodging with the agility of a cat. Sometimes, he would catch my wrist in midair and then shove me to the side.

He caught his first charge when he was twelve years old, about to turn thirteen. It was for strong-arm robbery, which is a third-degree felony. He beat up a kid his age who went to his school, and then he took the kid's bike. After he'd spent twenty-one days in Dade Juvenile Jail, Mima warned him, saying, "Angel, I have a friend whose son started off stealing bikes. He progressed to stealing cars, and now he is in prison for murder. You better see to it that this doesn't turn out to be your destiny as well."

"No, Mima, it's not that serious. This is my first and last time," he said.

Angel got his first job, at my friend's auto parts shop, when he was fourteen years old, but between work and school he still managed to rob and sell drugs. His love for money morphed and mutated into a monster, to the point of him dropping out of school because it didn't make him money. He considered school a waste of time. Not to mention he had a girlfriend now whom he was sexually active with.

I cried plenty of nights while he was out there drinking and smoking, doing only God knows what with his homies and chongas. Plenty of times I tried stopping him, but he would run past me and out the door while I was still yelling at him to stop. If I barricaded the door with my body, he would shake his head, smile, and retreat to his room, slam the door, and blast that 2Pac (American Rapper) music out of his stereo: "I see death around the corner." Later on, I'd open his door to invite him to dinner, only to find out he had sneaked out his bedroom window. I tried calling the cops on him. They would counsel him, and they even locked him up once, but he would get out and eventually go back to the same self-destructive behavior. Around this time, I had been sober for approximately six years. My program has taught me that going back to the same self-destructive behavior and expecting different results is the definition of insanity.

Angel caught his second felony charge when he was fourteen years old—just five months before he turned fifteen. He led a police chase in a stolen car, crashed into a house, and continued to run on foot. They charged him with armed robbery, grand theft auto, aggravated fleeing and eluding a police officer, and resisting arrest, not to mention all the traffic violations for running a red light and three stop signs, reckless driving, and leaving the scene of an accident. Before he even got his restricted learners permit, his license had been suspended. He pleaded out and was labeled a signal 150 career criminal. He was in and out of jail, drug programs, probation, and house arrest. When Angel turned sixteen years old, his father, Joseph, was released from the federal penitentiary on parole. He was living in Omaha, Nebraska. Joseph requested that I send Angel up to Omaha, so I did. Not even a month later, Joseph sent Angel back to me.

Then Angel met his match, Anastasia. At first, she seemed like an angel from heaven. She was a beautiful Colombian/Cuban girl from New Jersey with long dirty-blond hair, with measurements of 34-26-34 and a C cup. Petite but full in the right places, she looked like a little Shakira. She was keeping Angel out of trouble, and he had slowed down. Everything seemed so quiet and serene. A little too quiet. They say the sea is at its calmest just before the biggest storm. We all believed Anastasia might've been the solution to our problems. Boy, were we wrong. There's a big difference between love and obsession, and these two had a deadly mixture of both. Angel had always been a sucker for love, looking for love in all the wrong places.

CHAPTER 8

Love and obsession

The best way to describe what Angel and Anastasia felt toward each other was just Love and obsession, they were always holding hands, hugging, and kissing. They would meet and speak to each other like compelling magnets, joined together as if they were Siamese twins. They met through Anastasia's cousin Joe, who happened to be Angel 's friend. Angel and Joe used to sell pot to Joe's uncle Stewie, who was Anastasia's dad. She developed a crush toward Angel and vice versa. Before you knew it, they were exploring each other's bodies every chance they got.

When her parents found out who she was dating, they flipped out and forbade her from seeing Angel and Anastasia had a Romeo-and-Juliet type of relationship. Planning, escaping, and sneaking away to be with each other against her parents' wishes. Her parents were verbally abusive toward Angel . They called him a thug, hoodlum, rat, *bandolero* (gangster), and worse. You couldn't blame them, though. Angel always dressed like one, with his black leather hat/cap, white tank top, black or navy-blue Dickies shorts, black Reebok classics, and a casual T-shirt hanging around his neck or a collared polo shirt with the collar flipped up. Sometimes he'd wear a plaid short-sleeve button-up shirt with the top four or five buttons opened, exposing his tank top and silver chain. He was always popping his collar up.

Eventually Anastasia's parents gave in. Too much was going on. It just so happened that Stella, Anastasia's mom, caught Stewie cheating on her with one of his young female coworkers. Stella had just given birth to their youngest child five months before this, so she was going through all types of emotional and psychological obstacles and roller coasters that made her lose her job at the bank. She was freaking out, showing up to Stewie's workplace yelling, cursing, and trying to pick a fight with his mistress Fay. Because of that, Stewie ended up losing his job too. They were always yelling, arguing, and fighting in that house, and the baby was always bawling in the background. Stewie would leave with Stella on his tail, yelling, cursing at him, and asking if he was running off to sleep with Fay. They were so caught up in this tragic triangle that they'd often neglect their baby, which Anastasia and Angel practically raised.

Angel and Anastasia danced as partners at her fifteenth birthday party. Angel was sixteen years old at the time. Plenty of nights, Stewie would be out with Fay, leaving Stella at home in a zombie-like state of mind. Once everyone was asleep, Angel and Anastasia would make love while drunk, high on pot or ecstasy pills, or sometimes on all three. Eventually the inevitable happened, and she got pregnant. Together they went to the clinic, got her prenatal vitamins, and tried to keep the pregnancy a secret for as long as possible. When her parents noticed the bump in her belly and found out, all hell broke loose. They tried forcing her into an abortion but couldn't. Anastasia stood her ground and refused. She was RH negative and had been raped previously at the age of fourteen by her boyfriend at the time. Her parents approved of him because he and his family were jewelers. They were wealthy and would spoil her parents with jewelry. This man had impregnated Anastasia. Behind Stewie's back, Anastasia and Stella went to an abortion clinic, and Anastasia had an abortion, striking a deal with her now ex-boyfriend that this incident would remain a skeleton in the closet and that it would all be swept under the rug if he would just leave her alone. This was done in secret out of fear that if Stewie found out, he would kill that little punk. So, having another abortion about a year and a half later with being RH negative could have kept Anastasia from ever bearing children. Plus, Anastasia loved and adored Angel and wanted to be the mother of his child.

On the other side of town, Angel and his family were discussing the situation at hand. One day his aunt Grace was giving him and Anastasia a ride in the car and speaking from her own experience of having children at a young age, Grace advised the young couple to have an abortion. She said that they were too young and weren't financially stable. They hadn't even finished high school yet! She warned them of the lifetime responsibilities of parenthood and how their whole lives were about to change. No more partying, no more fun.

Angel agreed with his aunt. Grace dropped the couple off at my house, and Angel jumped on the computer, while Anastasia softly asked to speak with me in private. I took her into my room, and she poured her heart out to me. She expressed how much she loved my son, what she was going through with her parents trying to make her have an abortion, her concerns against the abortion because of her Rh-negative complications, and everything my sister Grace had just lectured them about in the car. She said Grace had persuaded Angel into agreeing with her. My heart went out to this poor, little but strong young lady. I understood her, and I backed her up 100 percent. Not to mention this was my first grandbaby that we were talking about here. I hugged her and gave her my blessing to have the baby. I told her not to worry about a thing but to wipe her tears, get herself together, and leave Angel to me. After she calmed down and regained her composure, I held her hand, and we walked out of the room together. We entered the living room, and I sat down on the couch facing Angel 's left side. He was on the Internet, focused on the computer, but I knew he could see us through his peripheral vision. I crossed my arms, leaned back on the armrest, lifted and crossed my legs on the couch, and got comfortable. Anastasia followed suit, crossing her arms in front of her chest as well, leaning her right hip against the armrest of the couch I was sitting at, and bouncing her left leg, which was on the outer side. I stared my son down, and so did Anastasia. I know him better than anybody except God Himself. I know his heart, I have access to it, and I know how to pierce it. Angel glanced at us, then looked back at the computer screen. He smiled, clicked the mouse a few times, sighed, and pushed himself away from the computer table. As the wheels of the computer chair rolled back onto the tile, he spun to face us and grinned.

"What?" he said.

I asked, "You are going to kill my first and only grandbaby?"

"Damn, why do you have to say it like that?"

"Because that's what you are doing if you decide to have the abortion."

He started to say, "What Grace said is true, Mom. We're too young; we don't have money—"

I cut him off.

"I don't care what Grace said. She didn't kill her kids, so she doesn't know what an abortion feels like! You didn't think you were too young to be having sex. You should've thought about that before you started. You had sex like a grown man, you made the baby like a grown man, so now you need to own up to your responsibilities like a grown man. And as far as money goes, *el nino trae el pan debajo de el brazo*," I said, using an old Cuban saying ("babies bring their own bread under their arms") that means God provides for children.

"Angel, did you know that a doctor suggested that I abort you?" I said.

"No."

"Did you know that before you, I aborted a baby? You were supposed to have a brother or a sister."

Angel said, "Nah. For real?"

"Oh yeah, and I couldn't live with myself after I did that. It's horrible for any human woman that has a conscience. I suffered and cried so much afterward. You don't know how bad that is, Angel . While pregnant with you, I was still taking birth control because I didn't know I was pregnant. I continued drinking, using, and partying with your dad. By the time I realized I was pregnant, the doctor said you might be born with birth defects or you could be mentally challenged. The doctor suggested that I consider abortion. Would you have appreciated it if I had gotten on abortion?"

"No."

"Exactly, because you came out just fine."

I smiled, and so did Angel and Anastasia, both getting my joke.

I said, "Do you ever wonder why I call you 'anormal (Spanish for abnormal)'?" I questioned with a giggle. "Because I told the doctor that even if you came out with birth defects or were mentally challenged, I would accept the responsibility of taking care of you as long as I lived, but I could not kill another one of my children."

Angel smiled with gratitude. "Thanks, Mom."

I told him, "Anastasia is RH negative. If she has an abortion, she may never be able to have kids. If you truly love her, you should take that into consideration and not put her through that. Children are a blessing from God! Who do you think you are to make that decision of whether that baby should live? What gives you that right?" I sat up, ready to shoot my final javelin. "Please don't kill my first and only grandchild."

He pressed his lips, nodded his head, and responded, "I guess we're having the baby then." All of us smiled.

Anastasia said, "I was going to have the baby regardless, but it's more comforting to know that we're in this together."

And that was that.

Around this time Angel was working at a welding shop that belonged to my boyfriend at the time. He had been given a raise and was now getting paid sixty-five dollars a day. He was living with me, but eventually Anastasia and her parents arranged for him to move into their townhouse and pay them ninety dollars a week to help. So, at sixteen years old, my son packed up and left my house. Our home.

Prior to this, Angel and Anastasia bought a car by selling a beautiful custom-made diamond-and-white-gold necklace and matching earrings that her ex-boyfriend had given her from his family's jewelry store. Angel was going to sell it to a jewelry store, but I offered him what he was asking for it instead. I figured this way I could kill two birds with one stone by getting my son his first car and getting a wonderful gift for my daughter Maria Cristina's fifteenth birthday. All for $1,000.

I witnessed my son go through pure hell with Anastasia during her pregnancy. She transformed from that beautiful, sweet girl into that girl on *The Exorcist* or Medusa. There was so much drama coming from that dysfunctional house. Anastasia would kick Angel out of the house every other day. He was constantly driving back and forth with all his property in the back seat and trunk of his Buick Regal. It felt beautiful to see sonograms of the baby, though. In one special sonogram, the baby spread his legs, letting his genitals hang for all to see. Anastasia was all belly, all baby. I threw her a baby shower at my house; we had a blast, and they received many gifts for the baby.

Then on October 11, 2002, her water broke, and everybody went to Hialeah Hospital. We were all excited. Although her water had broken, Angel Junior was procrastinating, so the labor had to be induced. Then the unpredictable happened. Junior was crowned. His head got stuck because Anastasia didn't dilate enough. She was throwing a fit, yelling and kicking people out of the room. I was the only one she wanted by her side. The doctor called for an emergency C-section, but they had to wait for either the doctor or the anesthesiologist to come from home. The whole time Anastasia was waiting in pain and losing blood. Then finally, after what seemed like forever, whoever they were waiting for showed up, and she was rushed into the operating room with Angel by her side. During her pregnancy he used to rub her belly and speak to the baby. Finally, the baby was extracted out of her. He was bawling. A huge, pink baby with a cone head, crying and screaming.

Angel was instructed by one of the nurses how to cut the umbilical cord. After he successfully cut his son's umbilical cord, the nurse asked, "Did you talk to the baby while she was pregnant?"

"Yeah, I always talked to him," Angel replied.

"Okay, put your pointer finger in his palm, and talk to him. It will calm him down," the nurse explained. Angel followed the directions given to him, and the baby gripped his finger with a strong, firm grip. This calmed him down, and the baby's screams turned into soft cooing.

Then Angel asked the nurse, "Excuse me, ma'am…he is beautiful and everything, and I'll love him regardless, but does his head stay like that? You know, with the current head?"

The nurse laughed and explained that the baby's cranium was like Jell-O, so a specialist would massage it and mold it back to its original state.

Angel Junior was nine pounds and twenty-two inches. He was a big, beautiful baby boy!

Meanwhile, Anastasia was in another room fighting for her life. She had lost so much blood and had become anemic. It was so bad she almost died. She spent the whole week in the hospital, recuperating on a high-iron diet. Anastasia had gone through such a traumatizing labor that psychologically she would never be the same.

It was not even a week after she came home from the hospital that she and her parents got into a dispute. Upon hearing all the yelling, Angel went downstairs to see what was going on and walked up to hear Anastasia ask her father for some water. Stewie replied, "You want some water? Drink out of the toilet like the dogs do!" Anastasia, infuriated, began to curse him out, yelling vulgarities at him. Stewie began to walk toward her as if he were going to hit her, and that's when Angel interfered, jumping in between them. Angel was facing Stewie, giving Anastasia his back and allowing her to place her hands on his back. Angel had his fists balled up at his sides. Stewie looked down at Angel's fists, stopped in his tracks, and stepped back. "That's my daughter!" he yelled.

"But she is the mother of my child," Angel replied with a firm, stone-cold tone.

"I want you both out of my house!" Stewie demanded.

Angel nodded. "Okay, just give us a chance to pack. We'll leave today."

While packing, Angel asked Anastasia, "What was that all about?" She didn't even know. She was crying and apologizing.

They packed up and went to her grandma's house. Then, one-night Anastasia got into a fight with her grandma, busting her own grandmother's nose and causing them to get kicked out. They ended up on my doorstep with all their belongings, but that didn't last long either. Anastasia had lost her mind. She picked a fight with me, accusing me of stealing twenty dollars from her. I got fed up with her and told Angel she had to go. He and the baby could stay, but the crazy young lady had to leave. "If you kick her out, the baby goes with her, and I go with her and the baby, Ma." Angel made it clear to me, but I couldn't deal with her, so they packed up and left.

By now, Angel had a different job, working at a warehouse loading and unloading semitruck containers for $7.25 an hour. He was also driving a different car, a white 1986 two-door Mercury Grand Marquis with blue vinyl interior and a Ford 5.0-liter V8 engine. They found themselves in their car in a parking lot with the baby in his car seat in the back. All their belongings were in the trunk and the back seat next to the baby. Angel's mind raced, and he got a flashback of a time he returned home and found Stewie sitting on the couch sipping on a bottle of Jack Daniels. Angel plopped down beside him on the couch. He has just gotten back from making a deal. Angel was experimenting with the dope game. It was dark in the house, and everybody was sleeping, so they thought. The TV was on, and Angel looked at Stewie. "What's up, big guy? I got my part of the rent."

Angel tried passing Stewie the $360 in cash, but Stewie waved him off. "Save the money. We won't be making the rent this month," he slurred.

Angel looked at Stewie, puzzled. Just then, Stewie handed Angel a check stub for sixty dollars. "That's all I was able to make at this damn furniture store," Stewie stated, referring to his new job that only paid him by commission.

"Damn! How long do we have until the rent is due?" Angel asked.

"About two weeks at most," Stewie responded.

"What about the family, Stewie? We're going to get put out on the streets!"

"To hell with this family! They could all end up dead in a gutter out there on the corner somewhere for all I care. If you love them so much, you can have them," Stewie slurred and then sighed. Truth be told, Stewie was hopelessly in love with Fay, but he felt trapped by his family and Stella's threats that if he ever left he would be up to his neck in alimony and child support.

Angel shook his head in disgust. "That's just the Jack Daniels talking. You don't mean that." Angel stood up and walked to his room where the baby was asleep, and he saw Anastasia standing with her arms crossed, angry and crying. Apparently, she had heard what her father had said, and she was cursing him in a low tone. Angel reassured her that it was the booze talking and that everything would be all right.

He invested his money in half a pound of weed for $300. Flipping that into profit plus his next two paychecks, he was able to make the $900 needed to pay that month's rent.

Anastasia interrupted Angel's train of thought. "I'm so sorry, baby," she said, sobbing. He looked at her, and she was balled up on the passenger side of the front bucket seat. She wiped her eyes and asked, "At least we still have each other, right?"

Angel opened his arms and softly said, "Hey, come here," and she comforted herself in his warm embrace while continuing to cry. "Yes, we still have each other, baby. Don't worry about a thing. For as long as we love each other and stick together, we'll get by. They don't understand you, but I do, so forget them. It's me and you against the world," Angel encouraged her.

"Me, you, and the baby," she corrected him.

"Yeah…me, you, and the baby," Angel agreed. They kissed and looked back at Junior. He smiled and kicked in the air, making them smile.

Just then, Angel's phone rang. It was me calling to see if he had found a place to go. Unfortunately, they had not, so I lent him fifty dollars until he got his paycheck the very next day. They rented a real cheap motel that night for twenty-eight dollars. Angel told me that his neighbor at that hotel was a bum. The bum had a grocery bag full of pastries that had just been freshly picked out of a dumpster behind some bakery. The bag was crawling with little bugs like roaches and black ants. The next day I found them a better motel for $250 a week. I paid the week and relocated Anastasia, my son, and my grandson to that motel, which appeared a little bit safer. As soon as Angel got out of work, he cashed his check, which was $290, and paid me back. They lived in that room for approximately six months.

Angel had finally stashed up $1,000 for the down payment to an apartment. He was able to save by getting his forklift operator's license, which therefore got him a raise from $7.25 an hour to $8.25 an hour. His weekly paycheck was enough for the motel rent and gas for the car. They were receiving food stamps and WIC, and Angel was hustling, nickeling-and-diming weed for those six months. Because Anastasia had choreographed her own fifteenth-birthday-ceremony dance event, she was able to find some jobs choreographing for other young ladies who were having fifteenth-birthday-ceremony dance events of their own. It just so happened that while Angel and Anastasia were at one of the dance event practices, their motel room was broken into and the money and $1,000 worth of weed were stolen. By some luck Angel didn't have all his eggs in one basket. The thieves missed a quarter pound of weed that was in the vegetable drawer at the bottom of the mini fridge and his pistol under his pillow. Heartbroken, they had to start all over again. At this point Angel felt as if he would never escape the "Telly life" (motel residence).

Even though the motel looked like an apartment complex by day, at night it was infested with drug addicts, prostitutes, perverts, drug dealers, and robbers. Especially on the weekends. God doesn't like ugly, and even though Angel wasn't an angel, he was doing the best he could to get his family out of there. I was working my program of recovery, barely making ends meet myself, not to mention I was on Section 8, so legally speaking, he and his family couldn't live with me. Plus, I didn't have money to give them. Anastasia's family was doing worse than I was. So, Angel and Anastasia had to fight and fend for themselves. They had to be strong. It's a hard-knock life, but you must hold on and learn that what doesn't kill you only makes you stronger. This is a world where only the strong survive.

As the man of his family, Angel wiped his lady's tears, hugged her, and said, "Baby, thank God they didn't find everything. I still got some work [weed] and our protection." Anastasia released a loud breath of frustration and agitation, but she understood.

To make matters worse, Angel had just turned eighteen years old, and Anastasia had turned seventeen. So, out of spite, Stella called the police and told them that Angel had abducted Anastasia and the baby. Now the detectives were looking for Angel . Anastasia's parents didn't know where they were staying, so the detectives contacted me. I assured them that this wasn't the case and explain the whole situation. Anastasia was infuriated with her parents. She talked to the detectives using my phone, and we protected Angel by keeping his whereabouts concealed. The last thing any of us needed was him going to jail on some bogus charges. The detectives told Anastasia that if she could show them marriage papers, then they would leave it alone. She forged her parents' signatures on the consent forms, and off we went to the courthouse. Angel and Anastasia got married while Maria Cristina and I witnessed. What a beautiful morning. The young couple was so happy. It was a spiritual moment amid all the drama that was going on around them.

Just as we were walking out of the courthouse, it began to sprinkle and drizzle a light rain while the sun was out. We all laughed. Anastasia asked Angel, "Do you know what it means when it rains while the sun is shining?"

Angel chuckled. "Yeah, I just married the devil's daughter!" Everybody laughed.

I invited them to the Texas Roadhouse to eat a brownie–ice cream dessert as my wedding present to them. We got in our separate cars and planned the rendezvous. As we were driving out of the courthouse, Maria Cristina and I were in my car, and Angel, Anastasia, and Junior were in Angel 's car following us. Suddenly, their car pulled into a gas station. What happened was that the newlyweds were teasing each other.

"So how does it feel to be married to the devil's daughter?" Anastasia asked teasingly.

"It feels great! Here, set fire to this!" Angel exclaimed as he shifted to one side of the seat and let rip a ferocious fart. Suddenly his eyes opened wide in shock and horror.

Anastasia exclaimed, "Oh my God, babe, that was gross. What? Why are you looking at me like that?"

"Oh man, this is bad. I just pooped my pants!" Angel exclaimed. Anastasia was cracking up in laughter as he pulled into a gas station and rushed into the bathroom to clean up, yelling on his way, "You see what you've done, DEVIL WOMAN!" Anastasia laughed so hard it made her cry.

When the detectives saw the marriage papers, they left the young newlyweds alone.

My oldest daughter, Julie, and her husband passed by the motel and gave Angel and Anastasia a wedding present: diapers, baby wipes, and $100. Two months after the robbery, Angel recuperated the money they needed. Eventually Anastasia's parents came to their senses. They received a backed-up paycheck from the government due to their mental and physical disabilities. As a belated wedding gift and a token of apology in trying to make things right, her parents helped a little bit with the down payment to the first apartment. Finally, after six months, Angel, Anastasia, and the baby waved good-bye to the Telly life and said hello to their first happy home, a two-bedroom, one-bathroom apartment with a nicely remodeled kitchen and living room for $725 a month. To move in, they had to pay a down payment in the amount of $2,175 for the first and last months' rent and a security deposit. They celebrated by inviting both families over for Thanksgiving. They purchased and roasted a twenty-eight-pound turkey, and everything seemed wonderful. Their love and obsession grew. The young couple fought and argued more frequently. Anastasia was jealous, calling Angel 's phone at all hours and wanting to know his whereabouts. His drug-selling business was growing. He was picking up payment in the hood. Everyone was calling him because he had that "fire," which is the street reference for good weed.

Anastasia noticed and always wanted to go with him. If Angel said she couldn't go with him, she would accuse him of cheating and throw fits and tantrums. During one of those tantrums, she punched their bedroom window, shattering it to pieces. Angel, fed up with her craziness, began to yell and complain that her obsession was so overwhelming that she couldn't concentrate on anything else. He explained to her that she couldn't go with him on every trip because, as the woman of the house, she had other things to attend to and she needed to trust him more. She was incorrigible.

"Look, Anastasia, look at the sink filled with dirty dishes!" Angel yelled, pointing to the kitchen sink. Then he moved over to the side and yanked open the refrigerator door. "Look at all these leftovers full of mold, Anastasia! We have growing, living organisms in our fridge!" Angel slammed the Tupperware on the floor, spilling all the rotten food all over the floor. He continued until the refrigerator was free from all the junk. "You know what, you want to break windows in our home? What am I supposed to tell the landlord now? Huh? You want to break stuff? I can break stuff too!" Like a maniac, Angel began grabbing dirty dishes and smashing them on the floor. "Who needs to wash dishes? This is easier and faster!"

The baby was bawling in the background. Angel was infuriated, and he ended up slipping on some of the rotten food and fell on the floor. "That's it! I've had it! This is over! You're crazy! Your whole family is crazy! You're driving me crazy! You've gotten us kicked out of everywhere. What else do you want from me, Anastasia? I'm trying so hard, but you're making life impossible for me, and all I'm doing is trying to make ends meet!" Angel yelled while getting up from the floor.

Anastasia was crying. She had a cut on her forearm from punching the window and needed stitches. But he grabbed all the money and his pistol and stormed out of the apartment. She ended up calling me, so I rushed over to my son's apartment, and what I saw was terrible. The whole apartment was in disarray. Anastasia was holding a wadded-up paper towel on her bleeding forearm. The baby was crying, so I held my grandson and called for an ambulance for her since she had lost a lot of blood. This whole incident got them kicked out of that apartment too.

At this point, Anastasia went back to live with her parents. Angel left Florida completely to get away from all the madness. He went to see his father in Omaha, Nebraska. After he'd been away for a while, Angel missed his son and wife. They made amends over the phone, and Angel and his father arranged to bring Anastasia and the baby to Omaha. After all, it was only right that Joseph meet his grandson. That didn't last very long. Not even two months after arriving there, Anastasia picked a fight with Angel 's stepmom (Joseph's wife) over how children should be raised. Angel and his father had a very long conversation about the whole situation. Joseph told Angel that Anastasia was very disrespectful and she had to go. Angel made it clear to him as well that "if she goes, the baby goes with her, and I go with her and the baby."

Joseph gave Angel some advice before he went back to Miami. He said to him in Spanish, "I want you to pay close attention to what I'm going to tell you, my son. I know that you're involved in illegal businesses in Miami. There isn't anything to start up there because everything's already been thought of and done there. Omaha is a virgin city. We can invent, build, start up a business, because there is a future here. I have a bad feeling that if you go back to Miami and you go back to your illegal businesses, they're going to catch you, my son, and they're going to give you twenty-five years to life. And that young lady will dump you, just like your mom did it to me."

"I'd rather all that happen to me than to spend another day here with you," Angel replied.

You can't talk bad about his mama; he just can't stand it.

Angel couldn't have been happier to be back home with his mom. Plus, he was infatuated with his city, Hialeah. He loved and was obsessed with Miami–Dade County. There was no other place in the world he'd rather be, and I couldn't have been happier to have my baby back.

He and his wife picked back up where they left off. They rented an efficiency on the north side of the northwest area, and he got his job back as a forklift operator. Eventually he got back in right with his connections, his brothers, and was back in the dope game. Angel was working a lot of overtime. He would wake up every morning at four thirty, shower, and be ready and out of the house by five to make it to his job before six. Most of the time, he'd have to work until ten at night. That was a total of sixteen hours a day, including his lunch breaks. By the time he arrived back home, Junior was sleeping. Angel would be so tired that all he had energy for was a shower, food, and to be with his wife sexually before going to sleep. Then he would do it all over again the next day.

Angel Junior was about fourteen months old, and he was already walking, eating baby food, and starting to say simple words. My son was eighteen years old but felt like he was fifty. It was starting to get to him that he was hardly ever there for his wife or child. He spent all day in a warehouse, making the next man rich while he was getting paid kibbles and bits. His supervisor was an old Cuban man who barely spoke any English. This old man constantly cursed people out in Spanish. Angel witnessed women shamed to tears by his vulgarity and men getting cursed out and quitting on the spot. And this man always talked to Angel with no respect, as if he was a child. In all actuality Angel was the youngest, fastest, and most efficient forklift operator the old man had. He taught himself to drive and operate the forklift when the supervisors weren't around.

The way he acquired his forklift license was somewhat of a coincidental miracle. It just so happened that there was a man in his thirties who lived next door to Angel back at the motel. He lived there with his wife and three children. One of the children was sick and had a feeding tube in his stomach. Angel and the man found themselves in somewhat of the same predicament, only this man had it a little bit harder. We'll just say this man's name was O. O. drove a minivan that had bad tires and was out of shape. The tires had slicks with bubbles, and the wire was starting to pop out. Angel saw this, and his heart was filled with compassion.

"Damn, homie, those tires have seen better days," Angel stated.

"Yeah, tell me about it. I think they'll last a few more weeks," O. responded.

"Man, it's too dangerous to be driving around with the kids in that van with the tires in that condition."

"Well, what can I do? I can't afford to change them right now. I have no choice," O. said in his defense.

"How much does it cost to change them?" Angel asked.

"New ones are out of the question and used tires in good conditions are about twenty dollars a tire including labor."

"Well, let's go get them changed," Angel stated.

"I can't afford it. I don't have money!" O. exclaimed.

"I didn't ask you if you could afford it or if you had money. I said let's go get them changed. I got the money," Angel replied with a smile.

O.'s face lit up, and he said, "Damn, but I won't be able to pay you back for a while."

"Don't worry about it," Angel simply replied.

They went to a nearby tire shop and changed all four tires. Angel paid the bill and invited O. to smoke a blunt. O. was so happy and really wanted to pay Angel back. Out of curiosity, O. asked, "How did you get the money? Where do you work at, bro?"

"I work at a warehouse through an agency loading and unloading boxes onto containers that are rigged up to them big eighteen-wheeler trucks, and I slang [sell] weed on the side," Angel answered. "How much do you make at that warehouse? " Seven twenty-five an hour, but I can get a dollar raise to eight twenty-five an hour if only I could get my forklift license."

"Really? Do you know how to drive a forklift?" O. asked excitedly.

"Yes, why?" Angel answered, curious where this was leading and why O. was so excited. Had he smoked too much? he wondered.

"Oh man, now let me help you out! I have a friend that works for Caterpillar. I can get you a license right away, but you really need to know what you're doing on one of those things, or you can get my friend in trouble," O. replied with a huge grin on his face.

"What? Really? Yeah, of course I know how to operate one. I've been practicing behind my supervisor's back. Wow! If you could do that, man, that extra dollar would be a huge blessing, believe it or not!" Angel replied in excitement.

"Ha, ha! Let's go get you a forklift license, dawg!" O. replied.

The process took only minutes. Angel signed, the instructor who was O.'s friend signed, and it was done out of the instructor's living room. Then Angel and O. went to the nearest Office Depot and had it laminated. Bada Bing Bada boom, it was official. Angel took it to his supervisor and in his Tony Montana accent, the supervisor asked, "Where did you get this? At the flea market?" Then he laughed out loud and sent Angel to the office building for his promotion and raise. First, he had to watch a video, take a written test, and pass to receive the promotion and raise. Angel passed, and things were starting to look a little bit better for the time being.

After a while, everything started to get old. All those hours in that dusty, hot, and dirty warehouse, away from his family, working for a temporary agency that was taking at least one third of his pay, if not more. He got no benefits and was on the forklift so long he could almost feel the hemorrhoids forming and building calluses on his butt from the hard seat. His nostrils were black from dust, dirt, and the inhalation of propane exhaust fumes. There was no more promotion or future. He was just stuck at this dead-end job with a disrespectful, nagging boss.

Then, out of nowhere the job offer of a lifetime was presented to Angel by one of the social workers at the temp agency. A bio scientific lab / warehouse was looking for trustworthy, reliable, hardworking employees to undergo a training period, and once they were proven efficient, they would be contracted by the actual company. That meant no more temp agency, a high pay rate starting at fifteen dollars an hour, benefits, and a brighter future. The temp agency had recommended him as one of their best workers, but one of the qualifications he had to meet was the passing of a clean and successful hair, blood, and urine drug screening. Angel had to let this opportunity slip through his hands. Unfortunately, he would never pass the hair tests. He smoked weed daily. For the first time in his life, he regretted smoking pot. This situation was deeply disappointing and even unbelievable. But you see, Angel couldn't stop because CaridadJane (another name for weed) was his first, true love and obsession. Everything and anything came after marijuana. Since the day he first tried her at ten years old in 1995 while hanging out with his big homies in the hood listening to 2Pac's "Shorty Wanna Be a Thug," he needed CaridadJane to cope with life on life's terms, to ease his pain and mined from stress, because when he didn't have her, he was miserable. CaridadJane was obsessed with him too. Since she met him, she had taken over his mind and life so that eight years later, she was hindering him from the chance of a lifetime, a chance for legitimate success. She had to be involved in everything he did and all his activities. Angel couldn't have fun unless he had her—before and after watching a movie, before and after intimacy, before and after eating, before and after sleeping. She consumed him alive. If he wanted to be successful, it would only be with and through her or she wouldn't allow it.

The supervisor had created a new rule that nobody could use cell phones while on the job. Due to Angel 's part-time side hustle, he often had clientele calling him on a regular basis. He usually put his cell phone on silent vibrator and let the phone calls go to the voice mail. Well, it just so happened that one afternoon Angel decided to entertain one of the phone calls out of curiosity. He looked around and didn't see the old nagging supervisor in sight, so he accepted the phone call.

"What it does?" Angel asked as he answered the phone call.

"What's up, li'l homie? I need an ounce of regs," the client responded.

"That'll be sixty dollars, but I'm at work. Hit me back up in about four hours," Angel advised the client.

"I need it now. I'll drive to you."

"I don't got it on me. Just wait, please," Angel pleaded.

"I'll give you seventy-five dollars if you can give it to me now. Please, dawg. Tell your boss you got to go for something."

Angel thought seventy-five dollars in fifteen minutes sure beat thirty-two dollars in four hours.

Suddenly, the old nagger creeped up on him, yelling at the top of his lungs, "Oye M.....! Cuelga el teléfono ese y sácame el pallet ese Anda!" (Hey, f...g! Hang up that phone and pull that pallet out!)

Just then the client on the phone said, "Damn. Who's that, your dad?" and started laughing.

Angel replied, "Nah. Listen, I'm on my way. I'll call you in five minutes. Wait for me, okay?"

"Yeah, for sure! I'll wait, call me."

Angel hung up his cell phone, jumped off the forklift, and told the nagging supervisor, "You pull the pallet out. Better yet, take the forklift, that pallet, and this whole warehouse and shove it up your butt!" He then brushed past the supervisor.

As Angel was on the way to his car in the parking lot, the old nagger and two other young Cuban supervisors were following him at approximately ten yards behind. Angel was aware and noticed that the old nagger was carrying a flat bar that was used to lock the containers. It was about three and a half inches wide and about a foot long. The flat bar hooked around at the top like a lowercase *r*. Angel unlocked the door to his Grand Marquis, bent down into the driver's side, reached under his car seat, and pulled out an all-black Ultra star nine-millimeter. He swung the pistol around, aiming it and stopping all three men dead in their tracks. One of the younger supervisors loudly exclaimed to all the others that the new generation of Americanized little Cubans were qick to pull out pistols. Angel simply told them he didn't want any problems. He'd stay quiet, and they would never see him again; he just wanted to go home to his family. Then the old nagger made it clear that Angel could never return to work and that he was done. A mutual understanding was established, and the three men walked back into the workplace. Angel got in his car and sparked up his usual after-work blunt to calm his nerves. He turned the stereo system up full blast and left the warehouse, thinking and filling his lungs with marijuana smoke as he listened to 2Pac's "So Much Pain." He glanced at his pistol, brought it up to his lips, and kissed it, expressing his other love and obsession, which was pistols and other guns. The protection and power they offered was an invigorating infatuation unlike any other.

Then he called his client and arranged their rendezvous point. Next, he called his connect to explain how he'd just quit his job and didn't know what to do. His connect commended him on his decision and assured Angel there was more money to be made on the streets than cooped up in any average-Joe job. He said it was about time that Angel came to his senses and get into the dope game full time. He advised Angel to invest everything he had on "work" (dope) and join the team. Angel accepted, and they arranged for a meeting at another rendezvous point. But first, he had to go home and break the news to his wife, grab some work for the client, and gather the little savings they had, which was practically the rent money and some extra cash they had saved. He then had to explain to Anastasia his plan of investments and no career.

As Angel opened the door to their efficiency, the sight was beautiful. Cartoons were on full blast, and Anastasia was feeding a happy little Angel Junior. They were laughing and looked at Angel as he opened the door with complete excitement, then joined in on the surprise of Papi (Daddy) coming home early! Anastasia and Junior screamed, "Papi!" Junior was clapping his hands while sitting in his highchair with his bib on and food on his cheeks. Angel walked over and kissed his son, and Anastasia stood up and hugged and kissed her husband, then asked why he was home early. He explained the whole situation, and she made it clear to him that she supported all decisions he made as the man of the house. He looked at his wife and son, sighed, and just let it all soak in. He couldn't believe he was missing all these precious moments and was truly looking forward to spending more quality time with his family now that he was involved in entrepreneurship.

Angel grabbed an ounce for his client and went into his safe box, taking out $1,600 he had saved. He served up the client and then met with his connection at a strip club where they were chilling. They all loudly congratulated him, and the connect bought him a drink. Angel gave his connect all the money he had. Keep in mind, though, that Angel, his connect, and most of his brothers had all grown up together. The connect introduced Angel to the plug (main source where the drugs came from) and walked outside to his car and gave Angel his work in a small black duffel bag. The work consisted of a pound of weed; a quarter pound of chronic, which is ingrown, higher-class marijuana also known as *sin semilla* (no sticks or seeds); and an eight ball of cocaine. The connect then handed Angel a hundred dollars and told him this was just to start off. "Break it down, flip it, and on the re-up (double the stash) we'll double your order on the front [credit]. If you prove to be trustworthy, you'll move up in ranks and we'll be giving you more work. You dig?"

"You already know, I ain't new to these, I'm true to these. I won't let you down, and that's on everything I love. Thanks for the support, homie!" Angel replied sincerely. "Hey, what are brothers for? What's up? You sure you don't want to stay and hang out at the club with us for little bit?" the connect asked.

"Nah, all those naked women are too much temptation. I'm a married man, fool. I got my wife and kid waiting for me at home. Plus, I got work to do. Thanks for the offer though," Angel replied, then smiled. The connect patted him on the back, and they shook up, hugged, and parted ways. Angel was worried, but he was happy to be going back home to be with his family. He had no idea what the future would hold, but he felt free.

As time went by, his struggle paid off. He built up his clientele and moved up the ladder of success in the hustle and ranks in the brotherhood of his team. Angel became a connect. He was always dealing personally with the plug, and they had become close friends, like brothers, after Angel proved his loyalty by retaliating and handling a situation for the plug. Angel became a loose cannon; he felt powerful and untouchable. They had crooked cops on payroll. Battles and wars with the competition and rivals were anticipated and embraced with excitement. Shootouts in broad daylight, fistfights, and brawls were a regular, and their strength grew. Angel and his brothers became a strong young nation dedicated to criminal activities. To eliminate was Angel 's next love and obsession. He was infatuated with it so much that he got it labeled with a tattoo on his chest, above his heart. It was his lifestyle. He moved from "telly life" into a four-bedroom, two-bathroom, two-story home. He had money to live comfortably without having to work hard labor like a slave. The work was hard and stressful, and it threatened his freedom and life, but at least it paid good. Angel had money to give. He maintained his wife's family and would help me out with some necessities as well, though I despised what I believed in my heart he was doing. Because I was working my program and in recovery for the same substances that I suspected he was selling, he always concealed it to the point that there was no proof. We couldn't say it for sure, but the whole family felt he was doing something illegal because he had more money than usual.

Angel 's plug showed him in a magazine that statistically the car least pulled over by cops was a Jeep Grand Cherokee Laredo, because when cops see cars, a certain image flashes in their receptive minds. For example, a Chevy Capri or Impala on rims = a thug; a red race car = a drug dealer; a truck = a worker; and a Jeep Grand Cherokee = mom and kids. Then the plug told him if he donated a hundred dollars or more to a law enforcement agency, he would receive a special tag and sticker. Sure enough, Angel bought a 1995 Jeep Grand Cherokee Laredo. It was clean as a whistle. He tinted the windows but not too dark, and he donated the money and became an honorable member of the Florida Highway State Patrol Association. They sent him a tag and some stickers for his windows. All he had to do was maintain his license and insurance and keep the registration up to date.

Angel "had progressed". He now had ecstasy and prescription drugs that were in demand, like Xanax and Valium. he had all types of marijuana and sufficient amounts of cocaine off the back of the brick. He was even cooking and making crack for a handful of clients that kept begging him. At the same time, he had also progressed in his drinking and drug use. He smoked at least as much weed daily as the average cigarette smoker smoked cigarettes. He also snorted cocaine until his nose couldn't take it anymore, imitating Tony Montana. He barely slept. He started smoking crack and cocaine crushed up and laced in his weed. He was eating the prescription pills and ecstasy like they were Skittles. He kept a collection of guns that had been stolen from police officers, including a shotgun. He had so many drugs, so much money, and so much clientele bothering him daily that it was all very overwhelming, sometimes striking him with paranoia. Angel was officially established and stuck—trapped in his new career of the manufacture, distribution, and delivery of controlled substances while armed. Not to mention his birth inheritance of alcoholism and drug addiction was in full throttle at its most powerful momentum.

Angel and Anastasia were back to their old habits of arguing and fighting. Anastasia was pregnant with their second child and was always driving Angel crazy with all the yelling, cussing, and interrogations. There were times when Angel wanted to leave Anastasia and her family so bad because they were driving him insane. They were problematic, tragic, and always ungrateful.

For example, Little Stewie, Anastasia's sixteen-year-old brother, was always picking fights in the hood, usually biting off more than he could chew and then running behind Angel for help. On one occasion Little Stewie was driving his parents' car and crashed into some guy's car. Since Little Stewie didn't have a driver's license, he fled the scene in hopes that his parents' car was faster than the car he had just crashed into. But unfortunately, Little Stewie had crashed into a Chevy Capris with an Impala engine under the hood, hooked up for racing. Little Stewie was driving himself and wasn't losing the Capris at all in the high-speed chase. The man who was driving the Capris was a known gang member and a complete maniac. He was approximately nineteen years old, and he was screaming and cursing at Stewie and even began threatening to shoot him with a gun. Little Stewie did what he usually did when he was scared. He called Angel .

Angel was in his living room chatting with a friend when all the sudden his cell phone rang. Angel answered, "What they do?"

A scared and panicked voice replied, "I just got into an accident. I tried to leave, but now I've got this crazy guy chasing me, and I can't get away. He says he's going to shoot me. I think he's got a gun! Hurry bring out the strap!"

"Wait, wait! Don't bring him to the house, fool! Where are you?" Angel yelled back into the phone.

"It's too late—I'm pulling up the crib. Come outside strapped! Please hurry!" Stewie yelled back.

Without thinking twice, Angel stood up and rushed outside with his friend on his tail. He pulled out what he had in his pocket at the time, which was an inconspicuous .25-caliber Beretta Jet-fire. He held it in his left hand, finger on the trigger, concealed behind his left leg. Little Stewie was just then pulling into the driveway with the Capri on his tail. He and one of his little friends jumped out of the car and ran behind Angel .

You always kept a bullet in the chamber. All the cocking back of guns was only for the movies. In real life on the streets, every second counts, and the quickest gunner wins. Angel observed the man jumping out of the Capri's and speedily walking as if he wanted to beat Little Stewie's butt. He looked first at the man's hands. No gun in either hand. Angel pocketed the little pistol and then held his hands up to hold the man by his shoulders, pushed him back, and yelled, "Whoa, whoa, whoa. Slow down, homie. My little brother is a minor, and judging by your facial hair, you look over eighteen, so I can't let you whoop him—his mom will call the police, so just calm down."

"That little punk needs to learn his lesson!" yelled the maniac, and he tried to rush Little Stewie again.

Angel pushed him back. "I'll take the fade, you and me one on one. You're too big for him. I can't let you put your hands on him," Angel challenged him, indicating he would fight in his little brother's place.

"Nah, I'm just going to shoot this up!" exclaimed the maniac.

"You are talking reckless now, homie. Watch your mouth! Well, go ahead then, we'll do this like the Wild, Wild West, you versus me. There are innocent children in these homes—no need to shoot this up. We'll handle this like cowboys. Just you and me. I challenge you right here, right now, pull out your gun," Angel said while sticking his hand in his pocket and gripping the small pistol, keeping eye contact with the maniac, staring deep into his eyes, also known as the windows of his heart. While Angel kept a stone-cold expression, he noticed fear and shock in the maniac's expression. Angel stated his favorite quote, "What? You thought they stopped making guns after they made yours? Or that God stopped making man after He made you? Go ahead, pull your pistol."

"I don't have it on me right now," the maniac responded.

Just then Angel's in-laws came out and ran over to the confrontation. Angel laughed with relief. "You're talking reckless about shooting up my home and family and you don't even have a gun?" He pulled out the small pistol and displayed it to the men. "You shouldn't do that, homie. If I was a less reasonable man, I would have shot you in the face a long time ago, but I spared you because this is all just a big misunderstanding. What we have here is a car accident. An accident! The kid didn't do it on purpose."

The maniac cut him off. "I was on my way to a race. Do you have sixty thousand dollars to give me?"

"No, I don't, and believe me when I tell you, I wish this never happened, but it already did. I'm sorry for your loss, man, but we can't change the past. We got off on the wrong foot here, and we are wasting time arguing. What I can offer is that we all drive back to the scene of the accident, my mother-in-law will pretend like she was the one driving, and hopefully the insurance will cover and fix your car."

That's exactly what they did, and then Angel gave the man some good weed, they shook hands, and Angel reminded the man about the innocent children in both homes and that he hoped those were empty threats out of the heat of passion from anger. The man assured him there was nothing to worry about. Supposedly that situation was done and over with.

This was all happening in July while Anastasia was pregnant with their second child, due for a C-section on the twentieth. Forty-eight hours from the date of the accident, Angel and Anastasia were hanging out with Anastasia's little cousin Lisa and Lisa's boyfriend, who was Angel's friend Johnny. They all stepped outside onto the porch of Angel's house to smoke a blunt, leaving two-year-old Angel Junior inside in the living room. It was an early night, approximately eight o'clock. Angel and Johnny had just snorted some cocaine prior to them stepping outside to smoke. After smoking, Angel had cotton mouth (dry mouth due to smoking marijuana), so he invited everybody inside for drinks. "Hey, I'm thirsty. Why don't we all go inside and get something to drink?"

Anastasia responded, "Why don't you just go get something to drink and come back outside?"

"I just thought we should all stick together, you know. I've gotten a lot of death threats lately. I just have a bad feeling, and I think we should stay together," Angel replied.

Irritated, Anastasia reprimanded Angel . "Here we go. Every time you snort that shit, you get all paranoid. If you're going to get like that, you shouldn't be snorting that!"

Angel was hurt and offended by her comment, so he simply went inside to get himself something to drink. Angel Junior was sitting on the black leather couch watching a movie. Angel smiled and kissed his son on the head as he walked by. Angel served himself some cold Pepsi mixed with Hennessy Cognac. As he drank it down, refreshing himself, he heard fireworks and screaming going on outside. He shook his head. "Little Stewie is always heating up the spot." He rushed to open the door. Angel 's assumption was that Little Stewie was throwing some firecrackers left over from the Fourth of July about a week back to scare his sister. To Angel 's surprise, when he swung the door open, Johnny was lying in a pool of blood on the doorstep, screaming, "Angel, they're shooting for real!" Angel looked up and saw three red-orange dots swirling from a red SUV. He rapidly ducked down to the side and slammed the door. Then, *tap! Tap! Tap!* Three bullets went through the door. Angel looked back at Junior and told him to stay down. Angel then whispered a prayer: "Lord, protect me as I protect my family." He pulled out a pistol, swung open the door, and blasted two shots through the rear window of Johnny's parked van that was in between the assailants' red SUV and where Angel was currently standing. The two bullets flew through the van's window and windshield and smashed into the red SUV. Angel rushed to carry Johnny inside, and suddenly, the firing began again.

Anastasia and Lisa began screaming and screaming. Angel ran outside toward his pregnant wife, who was running back and forth in a panic. She had her hands up by her head shaking as if she was waving with her head ducked down. She was crying and screaming, " Babyyyy! Help me!" Angel ran over to her and wrapped his body around her, hugging her and giving the assailants his back, using his body as a shield. Angel rushed her inside to safety. Then she began yelling, "My cousin Lisa! Babe! My cousin Lisa!"

Angel yelled "Dam!" and ran back outside under the hail of bullets.

Lisa was stuck in a fetal position on one of the green lawn chairs, screaming. Angel grabbed her, and just like he did with Anastasia, he rushed her inside.

Then he heard an agonizing yell from his dog Boo-Boo, his tiger-striped pit bull. "Damn, they shot my dog!" Angel ran outside, but the firing had stopped, and the red SUV had pulled off. He frantically looked around for his dog but didn't see him. "Boo-Boo! Boo-Boo!" And nothing; the dog was gone.

Anastasia called for Angel . "Babe, I think Johnny is going to die."

He ran inside. Johnny had collapsed from the armrests of the couch to the floor. He was losing a lot of blood. He had already formed a puddle of blood on the living room floor. Angel held his hands, pistol and all, to his head in disbelief. Johnny looked up at Angel, pale faced. "I'm losing a lot of blood. I think I'm going to die."

Angel placed the pistol in the small of his back. "You're not going to die, Johnny. It's just a shot in the leg. Calm down. Do you have any diseases like HIV?" Angel asked. Johnny shook his head from side to side, indicating that he was clean.

Luckily for Johnny, Anastasia's laziness saved his life; instead of folding the clean clothes she had pulled out of the dryer earlier that day and putting them away like she was supposed to, she just left the basket full of clean clothes on top of the couch. Thinking fast, Angel grabbed two handfuls of clothes and knelt in front of Johnny's bleeding leg. He had black socks pulled up to his knees, so Angel couldn't see where the blood was pouring from. Instinctively, he grabbed Johnny's leg and began feeling on the shin where he believed it was coming from. Angel found the hole with the tip of his thumb. He picked up a shirt from the pile of clean clothes, placed it on the side, and folded it into a long rectangle, then wrapped it tightly around Johnny's leg to apply pressure to the wound. Blood was still leaking out profusely from behind the leg. Angel felt around Johnny's calf and found a second hole with his middle finger. Angel then wrapped another shirt around that wound and tied it tightly. He then wrapped a huge shirt around both wounds and tightened it. Lastly, he tied another shirt on Johnny's thigh right above the knee to somewhat slow down the circulation. Angel gave Johnny a couple bumps of cocaine and helped him and Lisa up. Johnny hopped around on one leg and exclaimed, "When am I going to die? I feel better." They all smiled through the tears.

The police arrived, and approximately twenty minutes later, the ambulance arrived too. The police caught the guys that same night, confiscated Angel's gun, and took pictures of the scene. A bullet had grazed the back of Anastasia's neck, and Johnny had been shot in the lower leg. Lisa came out unscratched, and so did Angel, by the grace of God. The pieces of concrete that were chipped off the wall by the bullets didn't even leave a mark on his face. Miraculously Boo-Boo returned the next day. He had been grazed by a bullet on his chest, but he survived. Angel's dog always jumped fences, so naturally that's what he did when the bullet grazed him. He jumped the fence and ran for safety.

Before the detectives left that night, Angel asked, "So, you just going to take my gun and leave me unarmed?"

The detective responded, "Just reinvest and upgrade to a better gun."

Angel just shook his head. Fortunately, he had his other pistols hidden in the house.

The assailants were out on a $1,500 bond each the next day. Eventually their charges were dropped because neither Angel nor Johnny went to court or proceeded with the criminal prosecution. Turns out it was the same maniac that Angel spared the day of the accident. Even though it was all Little Stewie's fault, Angel got the blame for it.

No matter how much Angel did to provide for his family, it was never enough. He paid for all the birthday parties; restaurant bills of up to $300 in one night; utility bills; mechanic bills for the cars; huge, top-of-the-line tires; phones and cell phone bills; clothes and shoes. He even pampered all their drug and alcohol habits. Every time they went to Walmart for groceries, he would spend a minimum of $400, which was about two to three shopping carts full. Every time I'd check his fridge or cabinets, they were filled with food. I used to joke with him, saying, "You know you're doing good when you have four different boxes of cereal on top of the fridge."

He would laugh and say, "I don't know what you're talking about, Ma. I'm just a hardworking man trying to make ends meet."

Angel spoiled those people. He'd always been generous. It was very hard for him to say no to people, especially those he loved.

When Anastasia gave birth to their second child, a beautiful eight-pound baby boy, in the same month shortly after the shooting incident involving Lisa and Johnny, Angel paid for her to have her own private room at the hospital. It included wooden dressers and closets, a sofa bed, wooden table with chairs, fancy trays that included good food, juice in a wine glass, and a carnation flower on the side of each tray. He brought Anastasia a huge bouquet of sunflowers, her favorite flowers, with balloons that read "It's a boy" on them. On Anastasia's baby brother's birthday, instead of renting, Angel bought him his very own Spider-Man bounce house costing about $600. Angel would do anything for them. He took care of and provided for his family, no matter how crazy or dysfunctional they were.

I don't believe they ever truly loved him; they couldn't have—not the way they left him. They were just obsessed with what he could do for them, what he taught them as far as family unity and the fact that he could make something out of nothing. If he could provide for them, they loved him, or better said, they loved the money and goodies he accumulated. Once Angel got locked up and could no longer provide for them, Anastasia began going all around Miami until she found the next duck to fill in Angel's place. Then that family moved on, abandoning Angel for dead. He loved Anastasia so much that he was obsessed with her. In his heart and mind, he believed she was his property and that they would be together forever. They had overcome all obstacles together. Everyone tried to split them up from the beginning, but they held on and persevered against all odds. They stayed together, the two of them against the world. He would've done anything for her. But sometimes love is not a fifty-fifty thing. In this case it was always more of a seventy-thirty thing, with Angel putting in the seventy while Anastasia only offered thirty. As Carson McCullers wrote, in The Ballad of the Sad cafe and other stories.

> Love is a joint experience between two people, but the fact that it's a joint experience does not mean that it is a similar experience for the two people involved. There is the lover and the beloved, but they each come from different worlds. Often the beloved is only a stimulus for all the stored-up love which has dwelt quietly within the lover for a long time, and somehow every lover knows this. He feels in his soul that his love is a solitary thing. He comes to know a new, strange loneliness, and it is the knowledge of this which makes him suffer. So, there's only one thing for the lover to do. He must house his love

within himself as best as he can, he must create for himself a whole new inward world. A world intense and strange, complete within himself.

Next stop, Miami–Dade County jail, where he would be introduced to his new residence.

CHAPTER 9

The Jungle, the Beast Within, and the Method to the Madness

The sound of multiple click-clank noises from metal on metal registered in Angel's mind as the keys unlocked the doors and the iron bars swung open. The officer removed Angel's handcuffs and pushed him into the solitary cell. He was in there for hours with a million thoughts going through his mind, uncertain as to what the future had in store for him. All he knew was that it was not good.

The Miami–Dade County Pretrial Detention Center also known as the Jungle, is at least ten stories high and sits right behind the courthouse. The detention center and courthouse are connected by a catwalk and bridge right into the Downtown Civic Center. Miami is surrounded by such a social environment: people walking to and from talking on their cell phones; men wearing suits and carrying briefcases; women wearing business suits, skirts, blouses, and blazers, carrying fancy purses; hot dog and sausage stands on every corner. At least two of the city's biggest hospitals are also in this spot. There is so much movement going on as people are getting on and off buses, trollies, and the Metrorail. Cars and traffic are busy all throughout the day. As the world turns, life goes on, and civilized society orbits around this building, oblivious to the uncivilized world within its walls.

This Jail a Standing display for over half a century condemned with evil spirits. Causing many lost lives, consumed by the realm within. If the walls and bars could speak, their stories would be full of bloodshed.

The Jungle's sister is called the Dungeon, also known as the Stockade. These are the oldest and most brutal of all four county jails in Miami, since they don't have cameras or officers in any of the dormitories. Once you are brought into the cell, the steel-barred cage rolls, and the iron door creaks and slams shut behind you. Then you are left alone to fend for yourself in a world where the wolves and hyenas have already formed their packs. They creep out to size up new arrivals, asking themselves, "Is he prey or predator? White, black or Hispanic?" Usually every cell has its movement already in place. Approximately 70 percent of the dorm's population is African-American males, 15 percent is Hispanic, and the other 15 percent is Haitian. White men are seldom seen in the Jungle or Dungeon. They usually reside in the safer jails, like TGK, also known as the Hotel; or Metro West, which is known as the Motel. These two jails are third-generation style and have cameras and an officer in every dormitory. They're newer and cleaner, unlike the Jungle or Dungeon, which are infested with mice, rats, and roaches.

The officer runs the dorm in both the Hotel and Motel, in contrast to the Jungle or Dungeon facilities, where the cell runs itself and the officer only comes in the dorm to count and pass out food trays. When you enter the Hotel or Motel, the officer assigns you to a cell (Hotel) or a bunk (Motel), but when you enter the Jungle or Dungeon and the officer leaves, the inmates approach and begin asking questions: "Where are you from? Are you in a gang? What's your name? What do they call you?" If, after you answer all these questions, nobody in the dorm knows you or recognizes your name, you must get in "the paint." This means they'll choose an inmate about your same height and size who's part of their movement. He comes to the center of the floor in shorts and shoes with no shirt on. Then these young men shout at you as you fight each other one on one without reason or provocation. They're shouting, "Tighten up!" "Get there!" or "Get in the paint!" Crazy, isn't it?

I know you're thinking that the average, somewhat civilized person would ask, "Why? What did I do? Why do you want to fight me? I don't even know this person; why would I want to hurt him?" But you see, believe it or not, there is a method to the madness. Average middle-class to wealthy households usually have both parents present. They usually punish their children with groundings and verbal threats. In contrast, children are usually punished differently when they're raised in poverty, around drugs, and in gang-infested hoods, ghettos, or barrios, where nine times out of ten, one of their parents is dead, in jail or prison, in the service, or just plain out of the picture. Most of these kids are subject to verbal abuse or physical abuse, resulting in child abuse. Some make it out of the hood triumphantly, against all odds. The majority, however, become the product of their environment. It is inevitable because, while the remaining parent struggles to make ends meet working vigorously and juggling spouses around the youth takes to the streets, eventually learning how to make money from the older peers, thus adapting and embracing the street life. Street life is hard; it is also known as the concrete jungle. Hoodlums, thugs, gangsters, et cetera, are all children of poverty, products of their environment, and men of the street. While upper-class people look down upon these men, they overlook the fact that these men are simply playing with the hand that they were dealt. They're simply living life without an instruction manual or the proper guidance, trying to become successful by any means necessary, tired of being poor to the point of risking their freedom and life to gain success. Deep down inside, a lot of these men have good hearts; it's just that the street life is a hard-knock life, and the concrete jungle always ends up getting the best of them because the concrete jungle is undefeated against men.

In conclusion, a man of the streets, also known as a hoodlum, thug, or gangster, grew up around violence, was most likely abused throughout his childhood, and has resorted to violence his whole life. His second language is win, lose or draw. He will accept the challenge and fight; it's his nature, just like Chinese fighting fish or fighting roosters, also known as gamecocks. If the man fights, whether he wins or loses, he has just passed the test and is accepted and allowed to live in the dorm. If he refuses, that dorm rejects him as "the police" or "not hood," resulting in him getting beaten up and kicked out of the dorm anyway. Thus, came the saying "If you hood, you good."

Part of the method to the madness is that there's a lot going on in these thoroughbred (gansta, down for whatever) dormitories. People are fighting their cases, preparing for trial, smuggling dope and other contraband, tattooing, etc. If everybody's hood, life can continue within the dormitory without fear or confidential informants trying to knock off their time by secretly jumping on somebody's case or telling certain movements concerning the smuggling. The majority of the "snitches," also known as confidential informants or CIs, are cowards, weasels, and deceiving snakes. When confronted by that challenge upon entering the cell, their first reaction is self-preservation. It's been exposed that often the government has infiltrated these snitches to gather information on pending cases and drop operations; therefore, the wise street men set up the screen to separate the real from the fake.

Angel wasn't special; he had to undergo the trials as well. He had to fight, and he accepted the challenge the second it came up. Angel dropped his bags and got in the paint.

Even though Angel was hood, he wasn't a beast. He had some type of class and morals, and he was somewhat civilized. Alien to his surroundings, he fought when challenged, but otherwise he tried to avoid problems. One thing about the Jungle or the Dungeon is that it will either make you or break you. Courage is not the absence of fear. Courage is confronting your fears and taking affirmative action through your fear. Eventually, the beast within surfaced itself.

Angel had a lot on his mind. His wife had moved with her parents, and the house was the first to go. Angel missed his wife, his kids, and his family with a passion. These had all become such a horrible nightmare, it was unbelievable to Angel .

He was sleeping on a thin mat on the top steel bunk bed instead of on his comfortable queen-size mattress at home. He was sleeping by himself instead of sleeping and cuddling with his wife. Many nights Angel dreamed of making love to his wife, cuddling with Anastasia, only to be woken up by the rattle of the steel-bar door opening and officers yelling, "Count time! Count time!" Angel would open his eyes to the graffiti roof of the Jungle with a knot on his throat and his heart aching, wishing that this whole tragedy had never taken place.

On the other nights, Angel had nightmares of the morning of mourning where the whole tragedy would play over again but the ending would change.

For instance, after being shot, Manny would get up like a zombie and continue advancing toward Angel . Angel would continue shooting the bloody man, but he wouldn't let up. He would keep on slowly walking toward Angel like a zombie, groaning, "You killed me."

Angel would try to explain, "You made me do it. You hit me first; you were trying to shoot me with my own gun! You came to my home to f—— with me because Barry sent you! I defended myself!"

The bloody zombie would repeat, "You killed me." His eyes would be open wide in shock and horror as he kept repeating, "You killed me." But instead of the words sounding accusing, they'd sound disbelieving, like he was examining himself. "You…killed…me." These last words would sound full of sorrow.

"I'm sorry," Angel would cry. Then in a strobe-light fashion, other zombies would pop up one by one and disappear behind the bloody, zombie-like Manny. They were all known clients of Angel . Then Anastasia would stop out in front of the crowd holding their two-month-old child with Junior standing at her side. She would shake her head slowly from side to side.

"You ruined our lives," she'd say.

Angel woke up with a gasp in a cold sweat to the sounds of fists rapidly smacking into flesh as two inmates were engaged in mutual combat. He was getting accustomed to the occasional REC, a.k.a. recreation. Fighting was also a form of recreation in this world. Angel witnessed fights over the smallest things, like simple arguments over chess or card games, horse playing gone wrong, et cetera. He even witnessed two men stab each other up over a roll of toilet paper. Yes, they made knives, or "shanks," out of any loose metal object they could find. No matter how much I pleaded with him, Angel would only share what was necessary for me to write this book. He'd say, "Mom, some things are better just left out. Less is more."

It seemed as if everything was a fight. Angel was fighting his case, fighting off demons and nightmares in his sleep, fighting in the cell with other inmates, fighting with his wife over the phone, and so on and so forth.

One-night Angel dreamed that he was a child again, playing in his grandma's yard. Mima, Tia Lea, Tia Congo, Abuelo, and Tia Lea's husband all lived at the same house in Miami's neighborhood called Allapattah. While Angel was playing in the yard, Tia Lea yelled out, calling for him to come to her. Angel ran toward her, delighted because Tia Lea was supposed to be dead. She passed away from lung cancer due to cigarette smoking. Angel attended her funeral. Shortly after that, Tia Congo also died from cancer due to smoking cigarettes.

Angel ran up to Tia Lea, and she began pouring some thick, red syrupy substance on both of Angel 's hands and forearms and then over his head. Tia Lea began scrubbing Angel as if she was bathing him. Angel looked upon his auntie with adoration. He missed her; he wanted to hug her. She looked up at Angel and said, "Limpio por la sangre" (Washed by the blood), and she smiled. Then Angel awoke, puzzled by the dream but happy that he got a visit from his aunt in his dream. When Angel told me about this dream the very next day, I was ecstatic because I knew the meaning behind it.

As a mother of three, I tried my hardest to do the best thing. I love all my children very much. I've made many mistakes in life, and I understand that I'm not perfect, but I know who is. Once I began my program of recovery, I got close to my higher power, God, and I tried diligently to introduce all my children to God. I gave it my most earnest efforts to instill into them that there is a God that created all and that the Holy Bible is His word. I prayed that God would take care of my children, and I put my children in God's hands at a young age. My oldest daughter became a Jehovah's Witness; she took after her father. Angel and Christina took after me. They don't believe in religion; rather, they choose to believe in having a relationship with God. Angel just drifted away and stopped believing after a while.

Every visit, I was there for Angel unless he would ask me to miss out because Anastasia was going with Stewie and the kids. In the beginning Anastasia was being good. She got a job and was visiting Angel . Within the first five months, the state prosecutor dropped all charges except for the second-degree murder. Angel had a public defender who was doing exceptionally well. Anastasia and her family decided to hire a pair of private attorneys who did absolutely nothing. They dragged the case and then got caught in some real estate fraud, were disbarred, and stole Anastasia's money. This led to Angel getting stuck with the alcoholic court-assigned attorney who also dragged the process out by asking for continuances, which led to the state prosecutor adding three new charges two and a half years later after the initial arrest: (1) possession of controlled substances (marijuana) with intent to manufacture, distribute, and deliver while armed; (2) possession of controlled substances (Xanax) with intent to manufacture, distribute, and deliver while armed; and (3) possession of firearm by a convicted felon.

Angel's legs got weak under him and felt like Jell-O when he heard the new charges. He couldn't believe his ears. Angel knew deep down inside that the state prosecutor had had enough time to fabricate the case. Now with the drug charges, there was less chance that Angel could win, whereas before he only had charges of second-degree murder with a deadly weapon that he was going to claim self-defense on. The circumstances were really looking bleak for Angel, but this wasn't the beginning of hard times. The situation started getting bad when, only six months after Angel 's incarceration, Anastasia started partying and going clubbing with her friends.

Anastasia was giving Angel attitude. She was drinking and using drugs, making it clear to Angel that he was no longer in control. Many nights Angel yelled and fought with her over the phone to no avail, like a dog barking behind a secure fence. Anastasia began sleeping around, and she even slept with one of Angel 's rivals/enemies. Angel would call her every vulgar name in the book. Angel had a childhood friend he called Gorda (Fat Girl). Gorda came into the picture while Anastasia was tormenting Angel . Gorda befriended Anastasia to get to Angel . She (Gorda) started writing Angel, and they began to correspond, and she put money on the phone and then started visiting Angel . They'd been best friends since middle school.

Anastasia totaled the Jeep Grand Cherokee on her escapade. Angel would cry his heart out, pleading with Anastasia because this was all driving him crazy. Angel was in love and obsessed with his wife; in his mind they were supposed to stay together forever, "to death do us part," which was why he was finding it hard to register all of Anastasia's behavior—how she was cheating on him and always deliberately disobeying him. Anastasia was surely bringing the beast out of Angel . With all that was going on everywhere surrounding Angel, he just snapped, overwhelmed by it all, and he began indulging in REC more often, fighting at least once a week. I remember Angel coming to visitation with black eyes, busted lips, and visible knots on his forehead and cheekbones often. As time went by, I guess he got better, because the war wounds weren't as bad. It was always me and Gorda healing his emotional mental and spiritual wounds.

Then one day Anastasia made her last visit. She told Angel she found a good man who was good with the kids and that it was over. Angel went berserk, calling out all types of vulgarities and even threatening to kill her. Anastasia called Angel a monster and a beast, and then she told Angel she didn't want the kids to be like him, and she did the unexpected: she told Angel he would never see them again; he could only watch them grow up through pictures. For a while I was taking the kids behind her back, but when she found out we got into a heated argument in which she also forbade me from seeing my own grandchildren. Gorda punched Anastasia in the jaw and knocked her out, and that was the end of their friendship. Angel and Gorda fell in love and became a couple. She would do anything for Angel, and when I say anything, I mean anything. They became the dynamic duo, partners in crime, Miami–Dade County jails' very own Bonnie and Clyde.

CHAPTER 10

Running Backs & Routes: The Hustle Continues

Even though men get incarcerated, that doesn't mean life ends. On the contrary, they are sent on the wall behind the bars with different breeds of man. Some choose to lie down, take medication, and sleep or watch TV all day. Other men begin seeking God, learning different religions and spiritual beliefs, searching for meaning and their purpose in this world. Some men take the time to educate themselves and read books, while others use their artistic talents to make a couple of dollars by drawing portraits or making necklaces and bracelets from different-colored threads, the silver lining inside chips bags, and plastic from bags. The same crafty men also fix radios, headphones, et cetera. They don't make a fortune, but they live off the land. Food and canteen items become the currency in this world where some people are blessed with families that provide and some who are less fortunate must continue hustling.

Then you have the "poppers"—these guys keep things on and popping. They're always scheming how to smuggle contraband to get a taste of things from the outside world. These are the most profitable breeds of hustlers in captivity. Their main tools to get the job done are running backs and routes. "Running back" is the label used for their personnel in the outside world willing to bring the stuff to the popper inside. Routes are the means, plans, the way, the where, the how, and what the running back must do to get the stuff to the popper, those scoring a touchdown. It's insanity at its peak, if you ask me. The running back risks her freedom for money, and the popper risks his life trying to distribute the stuff behind bars. Nine times out of ten, the contraband consists of dope: weed, cigarettes, cocaine, ecstasy, crack, et cetera. But people have been caught with cell phones, MP3s, knives, cuff keys, porno, liquor, and even guns. Though it's difficult to understand, there are many reasons why. For example, the street value of a nickel bag of marijuana is about five dollars, but inside it can go for anywhere from fifty to one hundred dollars. One bag breaks down to fifteen "sticks" (a pinner joints a little bigger than a toothpick). Each stick can go for anywhere from five to ten dollars. There are approximately twenty nickel bags in one ounce of regular marijuana. An ounce of regular weed can range from sixty to eighty dollars. Every popper knows that you can't be too greedy; so, if they can make $400 to $500 off one ounce, the running back is happy, the popper and the rest of the smokers in the dorm smoke the rest of the weed…everybody's happy.

Still in his addiction and insanity, Angel was a popper. Gorda became his running back. With all the time in the world to spare and an IQ of 128, Angel spent his time figuring out Sudoku puzzles and at the same time scheming out routes.

Every time he landed in a new cell, it was like landing in a new puzzle, a new adventure, and before you knew it, Angel had it on and popping, flooding the roof off each one of the four different county jails. Even though he was incarcerated, instead of rehabilitating himself, Angel only wanted to get high and keep Gorda happy. Angel established clientele behind bars. They would send her money wires of fifty or a hundred dollars. On a regular basis, Angel even managed to send her a huge bouquet of flowers. Angel would go to any length to have his love and obsession, CaridadJane: making holes in the window during visitation to slide straws through; fishing through the fences with strings at the Dungeon because their visit was through a fence. Angel created a spear gun out of sewing string and a needle in a gun made from an empty roll-on deodorant container and rubber bands made of the fingers of rubber gloves.

One time during our contact visit, I saw Angel suspiciously covering his mouth with his hand while coughing. But he didn't even appear to be sick, and I knew those were fake coughs. Then it hit me, and I put two and two together: Gorda was giving him balloons. They were being discreet with it too, so nobody noticed. They did this in front of Mima, Christina, and the officers. I was shocked with horror. What if he died swallowing the balloon? What if it popped in his stomach? He could die! As soon as the visit was over, and we were out of the facility, I called in and told the officers that Angel had complained about his stomach hurting and I thought he'd swallowed some drugs during the visit. The officials took Angel to Jackson Memorial Hospital and checked his stomach. They found nothing. That sly little dog had drunk water to fill his stomach before going to the visit and swallowed twenty balloons, each about the size of a peanut M&M so they were unnoticeable. Then as soon as he got back in the dorm, he drank more water and threw up all the balloons like David Blaine doing a magic trick.

Angel began getting a lot of recognition within this new world. He had the heart to fight, he was a popper, and he was very funny—a young man filled with charisma. With Angel the whole cell smoked and hung out. They ate, and even if for just a little while, they were happy in the sad, broken-down world within. Angel had brought a piece of the streets in, but no matter what or how much he did, there were always the few that hated. The few that envied and disliked Angel . Most of the time it was his own kind.

There are four types of men in this world, and there is a parable that describes the four. This parable is called the man with the book bag filled with gold bars. It goes like this:

> There is a man walking with a book bag filled with gold bars. As this man passes by three men, he stops and hands each one a gold bar and then continues his journey. The first man, delighted with joy, exclaims, "Wow! This stranger that I don't even know just gave me a gold bar. May God bless him."
>
> The second man just shrugs and packages his bar and says, "Who cares? If you didn't do it, I'm sure somebody else would've done it."
>
> Then the third man exclaims, "What a jerk! You believe this guy has a whole book bag full of gold bars and he only gave me one? I should kill him and take his whole book bag."

The first man rebukes both comrades. "How could you say such a thing? For the love of God, you guys don't even know who he is or what the man went through to get those gold bars. He doesn't even know us, yet he was kind enough to bless us with something. Nobody owes us anything, so how could you possibly muster yourselves to say such things?"

Nevertheless, Angel continued doing what he was doing, but not even for profit. The very thought of not being able to smoke or drink buck, to get high or inebriated filled Angel with hopelessness.

Drugs and alcohol were the only things that filled that void, or so he believed. Once during a shakedown, an officer saw the marijuana plants tattooed on Angel's chest and asked, "Why you got marijuana plants tattooed on your chest above your heart? Do you really think you're going to be smoking forever?"

Angel replied simply, "High till I die, lock till they smoke me, my sh—— won't stop till my casket drop."

The officer smiled and replied, "You're not going to smoke pot forever. You'll grow out of that phase."

After three years Gorda chose to move on with her life and left Angel. Angel recruited another running back named Sherry. I don't know how he did it, but he eventually manipulated his young lady into smuggling too. From inside jail, Angel even paid for her grad bash prior to her graduation.

One day an older convict decided to give Angel some advice. He told Angel, "Young man, you have a serious case. You need to focus and transfer that same effort that you are investing into smuggling that stuff into freeing yourself. You're smoking and hanging out with all these dudes, but these fools don't care about you or if your loved one gets caught or locked up. I was just like you. I had a murder charge, but I never went to the law library; I didn't care. I was smoking and hanging out too, but when that trial verdict and sentence came, boy, did that hit me like a sack of bricks. They sentenced me to life and it took me fifteen years to give it back in exchange for a manslaughter plea deal that put me back on the streets. You need to get in that law library, fight your case, and stop fooling around, son."

Angel nodded his head, but it all went in one ear and out the other. All Angel wanted to do was get high and forget his whole ordeal. He just wanted to live for the moment. Whatever happens, happens; it is what it is.

Besides the lazy men, the crafty men, and the poppers, there are the men who read and study all the time. They spend their days looking for their keys to freedom or someone else's freedom. These guys get high from beating the system at their own game. Finally, there are the men who exercise. These guys release their frustrations and agitations through exercise. It is their outlet. They feel better about themselves, and their days don't go to waste. At the end of their days that didn't accomplish anything else, they've accomplished physical fitness.

Caught up in this madness, you can choose to better yourself or worsen yourself, red pill or blue pill, dig yourself out or dig yourself deeper. To each his own, but unfortunately Angel chose to worsen himself, thus digging himself deeper into the system.

CHAPTER 11

His First Nephew

Angel's big sister, Julie, had a rough childhood, but we won't get into the details out of respect for her privacy. She drew closer to her father, who taught her about the Jehovah's Witness religion. So, at a young age, Julie devoted her love, time, and efforts to God through this religion. She used to sit down with Angel and Christina when they were kids to spend some quality time. Julie would turn off the TV and read to her siblings out of an illustrated storybook called *My Bible Stories*. Angel used to love the stories; they were majestic. Although Angel and Julie have had their differences, Angel loves his sister very much and will always appreciate her for gifting him with the knowledge of the Bible.

Angel was exceptionally happy when he found out that Julie had fallen in love with a good and faithful man of the Jehovah's Witness community. "Ricardo" is a successful man who truly loves and adores Julie. He works as an RN. At that time, he was working with infants in the intensive care unit. A professional at what he does, Ricardo loves working with and saving children. Ricardo and Julie got married, and they are truly a wonderful happy couple, a match made in heaven.

Two peas in a pod. Angel was filled with joy, delighted at the fact that his sister Julie, after all that she had been through, had finally found peace, love, and joy. For this Angel is very grateful to Ricardo. Angel views the romance as a fairy tale, a true Cinderella story.

After living together happily married for a while, Ricardo and Julie decided they were ready to have a child. Julie got pregnant, and Angel's first nephew was on the way. The whole family was ecstatic, and I was thrilled to have another grandchild. The pregnancy went by just great; Julie ate healthy foods and drank Fiji water. The baby shower was a blast, and they were blessed many gifts for the baby. At the time of birth, everything went well, and little baby Nathan came into this world. He appeared to be a healthy baby, perfectly normal, but right after he was born, they took him away for testing and even had a specialist present. Little did I know that my daughter and Ricardo had found out through sonograms way before the baby was born that he had a kidney condition polycystic kidney disease. They kept it all to themselves and never told me or anyone until the day he was born.

After different tests, it was confirmed one of his kidneys was covered with cysts. To make matters worse, baby Nathan had a lot of allergies. He was allergic to dairy products, nuts, yeast, wheat, gluten, and eggs, and he was constantly breaking out in hives. The doctors said there wasn't much they could do; there wasn't enough time. Baby Nathan's life expectancy was unknown.

This news devastated Angel when I told him over the phone. At this time, Angel was in TGK, also known as the Hotel. He brushed past his homies and shut himself in his cell alone, pacing back and forth in silent contemplation. Then Angel cried out loud, looking up to the ceiling of his cell.

"Why? How could you do this to them, of all people? They love you! They're true to you! And you allow this to happen! You know what she's been through! She's served you with all her heart! Yet I that I am a devil, my two children came out just fine, and I thank you for that because they have no fault for my sins, but what fault does Nathan have? He hasn't even been given a chance to live yet!"

The dorm officer was drawn to Angel 's cell due to the yelling and the handful of concerned brothers standing outside of Angel 's door. The officer was just checking, making sure nobody was getting hurt. He asked Angel if he was feeling homicidal or suicidal, and Angel replied that he was good. The officer kept moving along, making his rounds.

One of Angel 's brothers walked into the cell and stated, "I just got off the phone, and my mom told me my sister was diagnosed with gangrene in her colon."

Angel replied, "And I just found out my newborn nephew has cysts in his kidneys. The doctors say he is not well and if it gets worse he might get a kidney transplant."

"Let's pray for them together. I want to pray, but I don't know how. Will you help me, please?" Angel 's brother asked.

Angel shook his head side to side in disbelief. "God's not going to listen to us, big bro. Look at where we are at; look at how we live. "Angel 's brother's eyes got watery, and he swallowed hard and asked, "What do we have to lose? Would He listen if we promise to change or something?"

Angel smirked through the tears with a snort. Then his light bulb lit up. "No. We can't make promises, but we could try to strike a deal, and you're right—we got nothing to lose."

Angel kneeled before his bunk and instructed his brother to kneel next to him. Then he said, "Bow your head, put your hands like this, close your eyes, and listen to the words, then say 'amen' at the end. Now I haven't done this in a long time so, bear with me, okay?"

Angel 's brother nodded his head in agreement. Angel told him to relax, drew a deep breath, released it, and then began, "Heavenly Father, me and my brother gather before Your throne as humble as we know how, on our knees, begging You for forgiveness of our sins. We know that You know how we've been living; we are not perfect. I am sorry that we never pray or read the Bible, but we are not religious. We believe in You. We know You exist—otherwise we wouldn't be doing this now. I've heard of all the miracles You've done when my big sister used to read me of Your stories, so I know You're a good God of miracles and I know nothing is impossible for You. We gather here, Lord, to beg You that my nephew's and my brother's sister's lives might be spared. You might heal my brother's sister so that they might all believe, praise, and glorify Your name. I pray, Father that You give my nephew a chance to live. I give You my life for his, Lord. Put his cysts in my kidneys. Take my life, for I have already lived and ruined it. Give him a chance, please, Lord, I beg You! And I will serve you. I will truly believe that You are real. I will dedicate my life to You. Please, Lord, we ask and beg You. In the name of Jesus Christ and the Holy Spirit we pray. Amen."

Angel 's brother said amen, and they both stood up. "Wow, I felt that! You should be a pastor or something!" Angel 's brother said, and through the tears, they both laughed.

"Yeah, right!" Angel replied sarcastically. They shook up, hugged, and that was that.

Meanwhile, on the other side of town, Ricardo stood over his son while he slept and firmly whispered to his son, "Nathan, you have to fight for your life. I've done this plenty of times with different babies in my career as an RN. Plenty of those babies fought and survived. Only a few have died under my watch. Don't you do that, Nathan; don't you dare be one of those few, please."

With tears running down his face, Ricardo did the only thing he could do as a man of God. He prayed and prayed to God to save and heal his child.

There is a saying that's popular with everybody: "Be careful what you wish for." Angel was so desperate for his first nephew's healing that he planted a seed by striking that deal with God and didn't even realize it. God works in mysterious ways, but God wasn't done with Angel or Nathan just yet. Despite that prayer, Angel continued living that thug life, but that good work within him had already been started. God listened to their prayers that night because God listens to everybody and everything.

"Being confident of this very thing, that he which hath begun a good work in you will perform it until the day of Jesus Christ" (Phil. 1:6).

Three months later Angel 's brother's sister was healed of her colon gangrene after undergoing an operation.

And baby Nathan survived his three more months. Nathan still had the cysts in his kidneys that were causing complications. The doctor said he would make it to see a year and fighting for his life as Angel entered the fight of his life unprepared and without a clue.

CHAPTER 12

Trial, Verdict, and Sentencing

After approximately three and a half years of constant court hearings and continuations, it was time for trial. Angel pleaded with the state prosecutor and the judge to bring the plea down. They offered Angel twenty-five years' mandatory time (day for day). Angel couldn't understand how they'd been giving guys ten years in with ten years' probation or fifteen years in with ten years' probation for the same charge, in contrast to Angel 's plea of twenty-five years' mandatory with no gain time. This was Angel 's first adult charge; he figured they would understand That he was in his home protecting his family. Angel asked for a plea like what they gave those other guys, but they declined.

In Angel 's mind, he couldn't accept more time in prison than he had ever lived on the streets. They would have to give him that time and take on the approximate $200,000 cost of having to take him to trial. As violent and brutal as his experience in the county jail had been, Angel figured prison was worse. Odds where he would never make it out alive without killing again and thus getting a life sentence anyways. Plus, there was hope that a jury might find him not guilty for

in self-defense. So, in his fourth year of incarceration, Angel and his court-assigned attorney went to trial.

The first day of trial, Angel 's lawyer cracked a joke that Angel didn't find humorous at all. "It's going to be hard to concentrate on this trial because your prosecutor is so hot! Ha ha ha! Hey, it's just a joke. Lighten up." Angel took that into consideration, and for the duration of the eight-day trial, he showed up high as a kite. Angel couldn't understand a thing that was being said in that trial; he was truly unprepared. Things were happening so quickly, but here is what he did understand: Angel's jury was contaminated with prejudice because the prosecutor's focus was to paint Angel out to be this big-time drug lord, which was silly because all they had was a Ziploc bag with individual baggies of marijuana and another one with Xanax. No huge bank accounts, no large sums of money or fancy cars had been confiscated.

But the prosecutors are professionals at what they do. They fabricated these horrible fairy-tale stories, labeled it as their theory, and you would be amazed at how easily jury members ate it all up as facts. Don't get me wrong, I love this country and its judicial system, but it has some improving to do as well, because justice is justice! I believe the system tends to be prejudicially biased and unfair so that some people (mostly poor) get harsh punishments and sentences, in contrast to the rich or politically empowered who get a slap on the wrists.

For example, there are plenty of men serving twenty or forty years in prison for vehicular manslaughter, but just recently a rich white boy under the influence of alcohol crashed into and killed four people, they used the ridiculous defense of "affluenza," and the judge only gave him probation, claiming prison wasn't going to help him or rehabilitate him. What about the other men who got all that time for the same thing? Why couldn't they get probation and programs? Or how about that man who was an out-of-control "crime watcher" who pursued, confronted, and killed that seventeen-year-old boy and then claimed self- defense?

It all boils down to how the judge instructs the jury. In Angel's case, the judge allowed the castle doctrine as an affirmative defense but then turned around and instructed the jury that Angel was not entitled to self-defense if they found that he was in the commission of a crime or a drug deal. In other words, they were sending Angel into war with a gun but no bullets, when in all actuality, the charges should have been severed, because the drugs were found after the fact and one thing had nothing to do with the other.

The detective who had arrested Angel got up there on the stand and lied through his teeth, but like I said in the prior chapters (which practically explained the whole trial ordeal), it's not what you know; it's all about what you can prove, and that's where Angel's lawyer failed. Even though the burden of proof doesn't lie on the defense, when the claim is self-defense, the jury wants the defense to prove their case. One thing led to another, the final arguments were in, both sides rested their cases, and the jury went into deliberation. While the jury was deliberating, they sent out a question for the judge concerning whether they had to check all the elements when checking the guilty box.

This forewarned Angel's lawyer that after forty-five minutes they had found Angel guilty. Angel's lawyer gave him the bad news, so he could break it down to his family. Angel had a bunch of support during trial. I was there with both my sisters, my boyfriend, both of my daughters, and a whole bunch of my friends from my program. Angel had his older cousin Rudy was there, and Gorda and Cherry were there also. The verdict was in; the correctional officers brought Angel back into the courtroom from the holding cell. Angel looked at us, pressed his lips, and then looked at me with a sorrowful smile trying to hide his pain and said, "I lost, Mommy." Then he sat down and turned around to face the jurors as they made their way back into the jury box from the deliberation room. The jury read their verdict of guilty for all counts except on the charge for some other pills that weren't ever present as evidence. The judge commended the jurors on their job well done and dismissed them. The bailiffs took Angel's fingerprints and escorted him back to the holding cell. Before leaving, Angel looked over to his crying family and said, "Thanks for your support. I love you guys, and I'm sorry." He pressed his lips and, filled with shame, he walked back to the holding cell. The officer told him he had to take his suit off and change back into his orange uniform.

This officer in particular—we'll call him "Mr. Dix"—told Angel not to lose hope. It wasn't over, he said. Angel still had the appeal process, and he had to be strong for his family. Angel nodded his head in agreement. The officer brought the suit and shoes back to me. I was in tears, in shock; my sisters were crying too. Everybody got up to leave, but I remained seated. Officer Dix came up to me; he gave me some words of encouragement and then asked me to leave. I asked if I could please hug and kiss my baby, my only son. Mr. Dix ran the question by the judge, and the judge approved if the proper security was applied.

Six armed officers blocked the door, and Mr. Dix went back to the holding cell to retrieve Angel . Angel was sitting alone in the holding cell when Mr. Dix snapped him out of his train of thought by knocking his keys against the bars. Angel stood up as Mr. Dix held out a pair of handcuffs. Angel assumed that he had to sign some papers or something. Mr. Dix handcuffed Angel's wrists in front of him and then escorted Angel back into the courtroom. As Angel entered, the judge said, "I'm going to give you about five minutes so that you can somewhat console your mother and explain to her that we're done here today but that she could return on your sentencing day if she wants."

I understand English perfectly, yet this man spoke to my son about me as if I didn't know the language. It wasn't that I didn't comprehend what was happening; it was just that I felt paralyzed, as if a part of me was stuck there and I couldn't leave without it. I felt as if they had just ripped my heart out of my chest, as if they had just killed me. After the judge gave Angel the okay, Angel looked and saw me sitting alone in the court with about six armed officers guarding the door. Angel said later that it broke his heart to see me like that. I was sitting down crying, hugging myself because it was cold in there. Angel said his first impression was that of a little girl who had just lost her favorite doll or best friend.

As Angel walked over to me, I saw my son as a man flash into his teenage years in a brown Dade Juvenile Jail jumper, then flash into my little toddler, and finally flash back into a man standing before me. I stood up, and he raised his handcuffed hands to my face, cupping it, and wiped off my tears with his thumbs. I got a flashback of when he used to cup my face as a child while I carried him. Never in a million years did I imagine this would happen to my one and only son. He kissed my forehead, raised his handcuffed hands, looping his arms like a halo over my head, and brought them down onto my shoulders, hugging my head into his chest. As I wrapped my arms around his midsection, hugging him back, we cried together, and then he told me that it wasn't over. He explained that he had a right to appeal and that if God wanted him to come back on appeal, then nothing or no one could stop that because if there was one thing Angel knew about God, it was that God didn't like ugly. He kissed me on my cheek, and I kissed him back on his cheek. We exchanged I love you and said good-bye.

"Hey, Mommy!" he exclaimed as I reached the door and turned around. "Keep your head up! Remember, one day at a time," Angel said and smiled.

He quoted a slogan from my twelve-step program of recovery— "one day at a time," which means exactly what it says. Don't worry about tomorrow; we live just for today; we'll worry about tomorrow, tomorrow. I thanked Mr. Dix, and the judge then exited the courtroom. The officers had to escort Angel through a hallway where we could see him while he could see and hear us. We all held hands in a circle, and as soon as the door opened, we chanted the serenity prayer out loud: "God grant me the serenity to accept the things that I cannot change, the courage to change the things that I can, and the wisdom to know the difference. Amen." That put a smile on his face.

Before sentencing Angel, the judge ordered a pre-sentence investigation (PSI) since it was his first time. Two Hispanic female investigators came to see Angel . They asked a series of questions concerning Angel 's background all the way up to what happened on the morning of mourning After a couple of hours, the PSI was concluded. The investigators later gathered all the information and put together a package of what they believed would be a just sentence. These investigators are trained, very highly educated concerning the law and the Florida sentencing statutes. This is their career, what they specialize in. Their agency was established to ensure sentences that are fair and equal and offer justice for all.

On Angel 's sentencing day, the "victim's" brother read a speech off a paper and at the end begged for the judge to give Angel a natural life sentence, which was the maximum that charge carried. I got a chance to plead for my only son's life, to brief the judge on Angel 's childhood, how he never had his father, and why the judge should give Angel a second chance. My two sisters, Grace and Victoria, talked to the judge. Angel 's little sister, Nana, explained how Angel was the closest thing to a father figure she had, and Angel 's little cousin JP gave a speech too. Then Angel gave his speech. Now, even though this isn't how it went word for word, it's very similar to the best of Angel 's recollection. It was recited by the very man himself for me to include it in this book. Here it goes:

"First and foremost, I'd like to apologize to both families for their loss. I'm sorry. Lord knows I never meant for any of this to happen. It was never my intention to harm anyone, much less kill somebody. The reason why I had my first kid at such a young age is because I felt I didn't have the right to take a life. You say I feel no remorse? How could you? You don't know what I feel. I'm remorseful all the time, and I must live with this for the rest of my life"—Angel began crying— "for the rest of my life, I must live with the fact that I had to kill somebody's son, that I killed somebody's father and somebody's brother. For the life of me, I cannot see how people could just say things without knowing, always assuming the worst and leaping to conclusions." Angel pointed to the quote mounted above and behind the judge and said, "Up here it reads, 'We who labor here seek only the truth,' but you can't handle the truth; you want conviction."

Angel turned his attention to the state prosecutor and continued. "With all due respect, ma'am, you spoke about what happened that day as if you were a witness and misled the jury to believe a theory you made up as if it was fact, but you weren't there! Nobody knows what happened that day except for me, that man, and God. I just want everybody to ask themselves why? Why would I shoot a man to death on my front porch? A stranger that I don't even know. Why would I throw away my life like that? I'll tell you why. He gave me no choice; he was relentless and incorrigible. He unlawfully attacked me in my home while he was under the influence of alcohol and drugs. I was in fear for my life. The minute he tried to take my gun, I defended myself, my family, and my home, my castle.

"I mean, what is this country coming to when a man can't be a patriot and protect himself and his family in his own home without the fear of criminal prosecution?" Referring to the prosecutor, Angel said, "You said there was never any physical altercation. The bruises on his face were from my punches, not little plastic chips off the plastic lawn chair. Listen to my jaw." Angel opened and closed his mouth, from which a cracking noise sounded loudly from his jaw hinges. "He punched me in my jaw, and for the rest of my life I have to live with this discomfort; I've been on a soft diet tray for the last four years.

"The bruises on his arm were a perfect match with the tip of the ASP. And finally, he had bruises on his wrist from when he reached for my gun; I grabbed his wrist with all my might to stop him.

"You said I wasn't in fear for my life. How could you possibly know that? Nobody here can tell me what or how I felt that day because nine times out of ten, you've never been in a situation like that, and God forbid you ever do have to experience what I experienced that day."

Angel looked over at the detectives. "And you, to have the audacity to come up here and lie under oath. Wow, come on, man...you know you coerced me and my family that day. You threatened to lock my family up and forced me to incriminate myself, sitting there with a smirk on your face. That's wrong, man. I've been truthful from the beginning. I even told you'll what you'll wanted to hear, and that still wasn't enough.

Turning back to face the prosecutor, Angel said, "You fabricated it into your own perversion and made up your own theory of what you *think* happened. I was even truthful about placing a gun in that man's hands after the fact out of fear, panic, and poor judgment on behalf of me and my mentally ill father-in-law. We were scared. We've never been in a situation like this before, but that doesn't make me a murderer. It was a simple mistake. I'm sorry. I'm not perfect.

"Then you contaminated the jury with prejudice by painting me out to be this big-time Dr. Evil drug dealer, which I'm not. I have a drug problem—always had it since I was a kid. It's a disease passed down to me by my parents. Like I said, I'm not perfect; I've made many mistakes, but my intentions were never to harm anyone. My intentions were to be successful. I just wanted to be successful. I'm not a murderer!

"So, let me ask one last question: If a woman decides to prostitute herself to make some extra money to give her children more food, better clothes, toys, et cetera, yeah, it's against the law to prostitute, but does that give the next man the right to rob, rape, or kill her? And if she were to strike back, defend herself, and kill her assailant, would that make her a murderer? I understand if I was out their robbing people at gunpoint, but I was in my home, with my family, enjoying a wonderful Saturday morning. I didn't go out there looking for problems; problems came to my front door, and I did what every man in this room would have done. I stood my ground and protected myself, my family, and my home. Maybe I didn't react like a cop would have, because I isn't one, but I am not a murderer!"

With tears still streaming down his face, Angel turned to the judge. "I don't have a written speech. Everything I've said came from my heart." Angel scanned the whole courtroom. "You know, I do have a witness that knows the truth and saw the whole ordeal. That witness is God, and I'm not a holier-than-thou man, I'm not even a religious man, but I know God doesn't like ugly. Lord knows I didn't murder that man, and so help me God, if he wants me to come back on appeal, can't nobody or nothing stop God."

Angel turned back to the judge and said, "Your Honor, that wasn't a fair trial, and that whole plea bargaining wasn't fair either. I would have signed a plea for ten or fifteen years plus probation, house arrest, drug programs, boot camp, et cetera, like the state has done before with others, but Your Honor, the state prosecutor has been vindictive toward me since day one. My one and only plea offer has been twenty-five years' mandatory, day for day, with no gain time for good behavior or nothing. You'll want me to accept a deal for more years than I've ever lived in the street in prison."

Looking at the whole courtroom while pointing behind him to indicate the jail, he said, "You'll don't know what it's like back there. It's brutal, barbaric; the only thing that's understood and recognized is violence. If prison's worse than this, then odds are I won't make it to see the streets anyways. I'll get killed or end up killing out of self-defense again." Angel shook and dropped his head in surrender, overwhelmed and tired. "That's it, Your Honor. I'm speechless at this point. Thank you all for listening. My life is in your hands now."

The judge looked over the PSI report and read it out loud. "The presentence investigators recommended twenty years, followed by ten years' community control, five years' probation, and drug rehabilitation." The judge shook his head no and threw the PSI report to the side. "I respect the jury and do my job even if I disagree with the verdict, whether they find guilty people innocent, guilty people guilty, innocent people innocent, or innocent people guilty. I warned you that if you lost trial, I would give you the max."

The judge sentenced Angel to a natural life sentence without parole, running consecutively with thirty years and concurrently with another thirty years and slammed the gavel.

The judge practically wiped his rear end with the PSI package report, completely belittling the PSI investigators, their agency, and everything they stand for to keep his word on a threat he made to Angel to coerce him into taking the plea. But what he didn't know was Momma didn't raise no coward—not to mention Angel was still in his insanity. This wasn't the first time he'd put his life on the line, and it most likely won't be the last. He's not very self-preserving, if you haven't noticed yet; the kid was wild.

CHAPTER 13

The Chain Gang, Life as a Lifer, Pain, and Tattoo Stories

The chain gang, also known as prison, is very different from the county jail. It remains a world within the world, only this world is bigger. From the county jail, Angel was transferred to South Florida Reception Center. There, they process the inmates, evaluating them mentally, emotionally, and physically.

It was still dark, and as the dawning sun began to rise, the bus rolled past the barbed wire fence into the garage-like entrance of the facility and parked. The steel gate rolled down behind the bus and was locked into place, securing the bus inside. A prison guard dressed in brown walked into the bus and gave the inmates a preparatory speech informing them there would be zero tolerance for nonsense on this day. They must follow and comply with all directions and orders that they would be receiving. Failure to do so would result in consequences and repercussions. He finished this speech by reminding them that they were no longer in jail; they were in prison now. The guard swallowed hard and then said in a hopeless tone and with a hopeless expression on his face, as if they were all doomed, "God be with you all."

Prior to this, Angel had been schooled by his homeboys to follow all directions because the officers were always eager to put the smackdown on any fool that doesn't comply and there was one on every trip; it never fails.

That specific guard walked off the bus, and another officer walked in yelling, "Everybody off the bus now! Line up and pair off, toe to heel! I want you to make the person in front of you happy! Let's go! Let's go! Pair it off shoulder to shoulder, toe to heel!"

All the inmates hurried off the bus, forming two lines, shoulder to shoulder and toe to heel. The officers counted them and then escorted them inside. Once inside, the inmates lined up side by side with their backs against the wall. The officers walked in the center, looking at each inmate. Then the officer in charge instructed the inmates to strip down naked, and soon approximately thirty men were butt booty naked. They were then instructed to keep their hands by their sides always, to face front, and no talking. The officer then clearly stated that even if their nose itched, they were to remain with their hands at their sides and that if even for one second, they moved their hands at any time, the officer would work with force because the officer would respond to that action as a physical threat.

The officers began checking everyone's tattoos, looking for gang symbols. Sure, enough one guy habitually adjusted his glasses on his face and was rewarded with a fresh slap in the face on behalf of one of the officers. All the officers rushed him, surrounding the man, yelling, cursing, and belittling him. He was frozen in shock and apologized (there's always one every trip—it never fails).

Next all the inmates had to turn around, squad down, and spread their butt cheeks with their hands and cough as hard as they could. I said all this just so that you can grasp and visualize the fact that this is the most degrading and humiliating thing a person could ever go through. Being incarcerated in jail or prison automatically makes you subject to shakedowns (a major search of your cell, dormitory, and person). On a monthly sometimes or biweekly basis, approximately ten officers raid specific dormitories, searching, flipping, and trashing your personal property, stripping everybody down naked and making them squat and cough. Then they storm out of the dorm with all the "contraband" they have confiscated, leaving behind a semblance of a hurricane's aftermath and a handful of cursing and complaining inmates. The rest of the inmates are usually institutionalized, already used to the routine and numb to the notion. They just quietly arrange everything back to its original state.

After the strip search at the reception center, the new inmates traded their orange uniform in for a blue one with a white stripe on the side of the pants. Each man had to get his head shaved with some clippers by inmate barbers. Each man had to shower, shave his face, and clip his nails. The nurse drew blood and urine samples from each man. Each man had to get fingerprinted and take an eye exam. They were all fed lunch, and next they received their bedrolls and were assigned to a dormitory and bunk. After being cooped up in the county jail for years, Angel was amazed at how big the rec yard and facility was. The food and canteen were better, so there was some relief to go with all the tribulations. For the next couple of days, Angel and all the newcomers had to go to various "callouts" (posted appointments) for mental health, medical, dental, and educational screenings. Angel even had to take an IQ test; on his first one, he scored 128, and on his second one, he scored 100. Angel went "psych" and got put on antidepressants, and he requested a whole bunch of vocational trades, trying to stay down south, closer to home, to no avail.

They put Angel on a bus to "the moon," from Miami all the way to Sneads, Florida, approximately a nine- to eleven-hour drive, to a psych camp called Apalachee East unit. This bus trip took two days because they stopped halfway in central Florida and continued the next day.

On the second day prior to reaching the institution, all the inmates on the bus where describing how awful this camp was. It just so happened that there were a couple of guys on the bus who had just checked in (been forced to leave out of fear) from this institution. To make matters worse, there were about three other guys who had been to this camp before on other bids.

Here are some examples of what they were saying: "ACI, also known as Gay CI because there's so much homosexual activity. They say 85 percent of this compound is infested with HIV."

"This camp is like a concentration camp. It's called CM4; there is control movement, and the officers are cruel, heartless like Nazis, and work the hell out of everybody."

"This is a gangland. There are so many gangs on this compound that there is a stabbing or a head bashing or razor slicing on a weekly basis."

"It's a psych camp. It's filled with bugs [crazy people]. This place is bad, man, really bad."

The bus pulled into the compound, and the institution came into view. A couple of inmates let it be known that they were checking in as soon as they got off the bus. The Hispanic man next to Angel told Angel he was thinking about checking in. "Man, you heard what those guys said. I think we should check in to. We got to at least try to get back to Miami. I didn't live this long to come up here and get killed in some hick town by some faggots or Nazi KKK. I don't know, man, what do you think?" this man called Poocho asked Angel .

Angel smiled his crooked smile and responded, "Everybody wants to be a soldier, but don't nobody want to go to war. I'll go wherever God sends me, and if it's time to die, then it's my time to die; nothing can stop that. If I survive, then this too shall pass. Besides, I'd rather die like a man than live like a coward." Angel was somewhat concerned, and he had butterflies, but checking in was not an option.

Poocho liked that response, so they went through with the orientation and security searches. Luckily, they both were assigned to the same dorm in a butterfly-type building. These dorms each had thirty-two cells—sixteen on the second tier and sixteen on the bottom tier—and each cell held two men. Poocho was assigned to a cell on the bottom floor. His roommate was a Cuban man they called Big Laz.

Angel was assigned to a cell on the upper tier. His roommate was a young Dominican man they called P Legend. Young P Legend had a lot of power at the camp and a reputation that demanded respect; he was the ringleader of a known gang and had a lot of soldiers under his command. P Legend started to question Angel . "Where are you from?"

"Miami," Angel replied.

"Tu eres Latino?" (Are you Latin?) P Legend asked.

Angel nodded yes. "Soy Cubano" (I am Cuban).

Angel looked at the Legend, confused, and asked, "Where are you from?"

"Orlando but originally from Chicago," replied P Legend.

Angel smirked his crooked smile. "In Miami we're enemies. We are rival sets, and we've been at war since the early 2000s," Angel explained. P Legend stood with a confused expression on his face.

Suddenly, they called for chow through the PA. Angel walked past P Legend and met up with Pooch downstairs. He was with a Cuban man named Eric. On the way back from chow, Eric talked with the dorm's laundry man, putting in an order for fresh blues and white, accommodating both Angel and Poocho.

Upon entering the dorm, Angel felt the tension. He looked up to his cell and saw people in it. Also coming from the room was noises of rapid release from quick exhaling that sounded like air escaping a tire, the type that boxers make with their noses while sparring, training, or fighting. Angel walked up the stairs to his cell. He knew what time it was. As Angel reached his cell door, he quickly observed that there were three unarmed men in his cell: P Legend, Black Boy, and Gusto.

They were in shorts, without shirts, and with boots. They had a "weight bag" (a bag of books used to work out) in the middle of the cell. It was set up with a bunk bed to the right, with two lockers under the bottom bunk. To the left was the wall, approximately nine feet from the entrance, and once you passed the bunks on that wall, to the left there was a stainless-steel toilet, sink, and mirror. Past the toilet there was some floor space about six by five feet, and on the back wall there was a rectangular window with a bar going down the middle.

Gusto was posted up with his back against the wall to the left; Black Boy was sitting on the bottom bunk (P Legend's bunk), reclining with his back on the wall to the right; and P Legend was in the middle of the cell with his hands wrapped with Ace bandages, acting as if he'd just done a set on the weight bag. Recognizing that Angel had returned and was standing at the entrance, P Legend said, "What's up, *parnita* [partner]? We're just working out and training."

Angel smirked with his crooked smile, walk past them, and put his back to the wall with a rectangular window. "So, what they do?"

P Legend smiled. "Gusto over here says he's from around your way, and I hear y'all boys from Miami be bumping [fighting]. I hear Dade County jail is one of the most ruthless, violent, and barbaric jails in the state of Florida. How long were you in the county?"

Angel replied, "Four years, and yeah, it's pretty rough."

P Legend said, "No por nada, parnita. [Not for nothing, little partner.] I want to see where your hands are at. I want to see if you're bumping, so what's up? You are bumping?"

Without hesitation and filled with adrenaline, Angel took his shirt off, throws it on his top rack, and said, "I am not the Baddest man in the world, but I'm bumping. What's up? Who got pressure? Tighten up."

P Legend smiled and said, "Isn't no pressure, homie. We just want to see if you are bumping'. Go ahead, pick one."

Angel replied, "I don't pick faces, all right…whoever, so whichever one of y'all want to bump, just get there."

"Go ahead, just pick one," P Legend insisted.

"Well, if I got to pick, I'll pick the biggest one. Tighten up, Gusto," Angel challenged him.

Gusto stood approximately six feet tall and weighed two hundred pounds. He was a big Chico (Hispanic) with gold teeth and a body covered with tattoos. Angel was five feet nine and 156 pounds. Gusto was caught off guard and surprised by Angel 's challenge. "Who, me? Damn, parnita, we home team," Gusto stated.

"Hey, nothing personal. You're just the biggest one, homie," was Angel 's reply.

P Legend snapped on Gusto. "Tighten up, nigga!" Gusto put on a serious face and began to advance to Angel with this set (fighting stance) up. Angel threw his fighting stance up, and as soon as Gusto passed the threshold of the bunks and toilet, Angel unleashed. Straight jabs—right, left, right, left, right, left—as fast as he could, tagging Gusto in the face. Gusto brought his forearms up to block his face. He was stunned. Angel sidestepped to his left, now standing at Gusto's right side instead of right in front of him. Angel connected a left hook that sent Gusto onto the left wall. The toilet bent his legs, forcing Gusto to sit on the toilet with his arms protecting his face and head. Gusto began yelling, "Chill, nigga! Chill!"

Angel backed up. P Legend and Black Boy were laughing at Gusto, who brought his hands down and exclaimed with a goofy laugh, "This little Chico's a Mack truck! Ha ha ha!" Angel couldn't help but laugh himself. This guy Gusto wasn't as dangerous as he appeared; he was a goofball.

P Legend looked at Angel and said, "Damn, little homie, I like how you fight. You have the street fighter style. It's freestyle; I like it. What's up? You want to go a few rounds with me? Friendly fade, friendly fade."

"It's only right. Let's bang!" was Angel 's response.

They squared off and commenced the pumping. They fought toe to toe, blow for blow, for three rounds. Black Boy separated them every time they locked up or wrapped up for wrestling. It abruptly ended when

Angel busted P Legend's nose. P Legend had blood leaking out of his nose profusely. Angel 's lower lip was busted on the left side. Black Boy said, "That's it. You both did good. Now shake and embrace. It's over."

Angel shook P Legend's hand, and they embraced, patted each other's back, and laughed. "That was fun," P Legend said.

"Yeah, it was. It's a stress reliever and helps blow off steam, plus we represent," Angel replied.

"Welcome to the dorm. I'm glad I finally got a Hispanic Bunkie that's bumping'. Even though we're rivals sets, we got to live here together now," P Legend responded.

"Hey, you respect my crown, and I respect yours. De todas formas somos latinos Acere" (Either way we're Latin, homie).

Eric, Poocho, and Big Laz stood at the door. Eric said, "This is just great! Now why don't you two just kiss and make up."

They all laughed, and then Eric said, "Ya deja la muchacha y comedura de mierda limpianze y bajen para mi cuarto para que se hechen una tazita de café y fumen un cigarrito." (Stop acting like jits, stop eating sh———. Clean up and come downstairs to my room to have some coffee and smoke some cigarettes.)

Within his first eight hours, Angel had to fight twice, but this gave him recognition throughout the whole compound. Angel and P Legend became close as bunkies, and a bunch of older Cubans like Eric accepted Angel as their own and embraced him. They schooled Angel on prison life—the dos and don'ts, and how to live a prison life as a lifer. These old-timers had been down for twenty-five, twenty-eight, and even thirty years. These were Cubans who came in the eighties in the time of the Mariel boatlift, also known as the Scarface days.

Eric explained the whole appeal process to Angel . Angel, ignorant of the law, believed he had plenty of appeals and time. To the contrary, Angel learned that after his direct appeal, he had two years and only two years to file for his 3.850, "ineffective assistance of counsel." The appeals following his 3.850 were state habeas corpus, which had to be filed within a year after the final decision on his direct appeals but could only be filed after the 3.850 remedy had been exhausted. That one-year time for both the state and the fed habe run within the two-year time bar of the 3.850. So technically speaking, to not get time barred and kicked out of the courts,

Angel only had five months after his direct appeal to prepare and file his 3.850 to stop the clock for his state and federal habe.

If that 3.850 were to get denied, Angel would have five months to prepare and file the state habe, thus stopping the clock for his fed habe. While the state habe was in the courts, Angel would have to vigorously work on his state habe so that if the state habe was to get denied, he could enter his motion for relief with the fed habe, having two months to spare just in case of any technical difficulties. The system provided Angel with a public defender for his direct appeal and his 3.850, and that was it. After that, Angel would have to teach himself the law, or his family would have to hire an attorney.

All this new knowledge was confusing and baffling to Angel . On top of that, the old-timers explained that if the prosecutor or judge hadn't violated Angel 's constitutional rights during trial, then the appeals would be in vain because that was the only thing you could appeal for—prejudice, fundamental error, anything that would have affected your constitutional right to a fair trial. They explained to Angel that 90 percent of appeals get battered down and only 10 percent go back and give freedom and time back.

"Look, all of us, we came in young, believing we would go home on appeal. A lot of our appeals are over, and we will never see the streets again. We'll die in prison unless the parole board releases us, and those people are a joke; they don't release anybody. So, don't get your hopes up, kid. Nine times out of ten, you will die in prison. So, in time of war, remember your only friend is your knife. Represent, and pave the way for your next generation like we've done for yall."

They say the most dangerous man in this world is the one who believes he has nothing to lose. Even though Angel had lost a lot, he still had his family support, and his appeal process was just getting started. In the meantime, Angel would slowly teach himself the law and focus on how to hustle to make some money on the side and how to get high or drunk. Angel learned a new hustle as a ticket writer, writing for the biggest ticket man on the compound, Big Laz. Big Laz had multiple life sentences that he had given back, but he was stuck with forty years left on his sentence. He had been down eighteen years already, and all his appeals were over with. All he had left was a 3.800 motion for correction of the illegal sentence.

Big Laz was a Cuban man thirty-eight-year-old and approximately six feet, two inches and 282 pounds. He was covered with tattoos and had an honorable reputation in prison. An honorable reputation in prison means that a man has his word, doesn't engage in homosexual activities, doesn't do dirt, isn't a confidential informant (snitch), and is a warrior.

The ticket game is like a lottery inside this world. It's based on football, basketball, and sometimes even baseball or NASCAR. The most money is made off professional and college football, and then basketball (professional). The way the ticket system works is, when very weak teams face off it's usually obvious who might win, so Vegas puts out a spread, which makes the odds more interesting by rewarding the underdog with extra points on the ticket. To play a ticket, someone must pick a minimum of four teams, and if all four of his teams win and cover the points, then he hits, winning at least ten dollars for every dollar he puts on his ticket. If only one team out of his four picks loses or doesn't cover the point spread, his ticket is dead, and he loses.

It's a big hype every year, every season; the ticket game fills the chain gang with life. The ticket writers make twenty-five cents off every dollar they write off. Big Laz was raised in Hialeah, Miami–Dade County, so he and Angel hit it off quick and became like brothers. Big Laz used to call Angel "the golden child" because Angel was his best writer. On a weekly basis, Angel wrote fifty to eighty dollars. On his best week, he wrote $195, cutting $48.75 to his own pocket.

Besides the ticket game, Big Laz, Angel, P Legend, and Poocho opened poker tables. Deep down inside, Poocho was filled with envy. He was another Judas. Poocho was sentenced to forty years at forty years old; that's practically a life sentence. Poocho's goal was to get down south and escape. After escaping, he planned to return to Cuba. With a gold tooth for a fang on his left side and tattoos, he knew how to talk the talk. Poocho had everybody fooled into thinking that he was a thoroughbred, but he was a confidential informant the whole time. To get a transfer down south, he informed the police that Big Laz had a cell phone. The sergeant and another officer rushed into the dorm, heading straight toward Big Laz and Poocho's room. Big Laz noticed when they came in that he was a it. With no time to do anything else, Big Laz flushed the phone wrapped in a plastic bag inside of a yellow Top tobacco pouch.

They locked Big Laz up, and then they stayed with Poocho in the room. Peanuts lived in the cell next to Poocho and Big Laz, and he heard Poocho giving the information on the fact that the cell phone got flushed and that P Legend had a knife stashed in a certain area. Officers escorted Poocho out of the dorm and put him in protective management. The officers found the knife and locked up P Legend.

The very next day, Angel went and spoke to the compound's inmate plumber. Angel informed him that the cell phone might get caught in the trap. If so, he needed to make it disappear so that Big Laz wouldn't get charged. Sure enough, the officers summoned the inmate plumber, and they went out to the trap. The officers were looking for a cellular phone, but Chino knew it was in a yellow Top pouch. So, while the officers observed Chino, that inmate plumber had his hands rummaging around in the filth. When he saw a yellow pouch, he forced it through the piping, making it disappear, forever gone. Without the cell phone, Laz was let out of the box, and Poocho's transfer was denied. P Legend got CM (Maximum Security prison) for the knife. His mother came to see him as a surprise, but they turned the lady around. Crying her heart out, she returned home.

The authorities notified Poocho that he would be returning to the general population. Poocho cut himself, staging a suicide attempt. Poocho had everybody so fooled that nobody could believe it, not even Angel . Prior to this dilemma, Poocho asked Angel to initiate him into Angel 's brotherhood, and Angel did. So, all of Legend's brothers stepped to Angel and told him that if Poocho was released back into the general population, then it was Angel 's responsibility to x out (terminate) Poocho.

Angel doesn't like people ordering him around, so he let them know that he wasn't a push button or a crash dummy, that he'd move when he saw fit, and that if he was going to do something it would come from his heart, not because they said so. It would happen after his upcoming visit on Christmas because Angel had a promise to keep; he had given me his word that he would stay out of trouble so that I could see him and be with him for Christmas.

Poocho was released out onto the compound. Everybody knew what he had done. Things hadn't gone the way he had planned. While in the county, Angel had read plenty of books, including his favorite Mafia books by Mario Puzo, plus he had Eric and all the old-timers as advisors, and these guys know all the tricks to the trade. A first Poocho wouldn't come out of his dormitory. Eventually he had to go eat, but that was the only time he left his dorm, to go to chow. A couple of weeks went by, and Poocho remained untouched. Angel made it clear to Poocho that nothing was going to happen to him, that he was straight. There was no proof that he committed the treason. Eventually Poocho came out, and with Angel he felt safe. Angel made it appear to everybody that Poocho was his brother and that, until they had proof of the treason, nobody could touch him.

Angel went to his visit. We had a great time, but I could see he was edgy, concerned. Though he was with us, his mind was constantly churning, thinking, plotting. He would drift away. We fed him good and took pictures, and I was proud that he kept his word to me by staying out of trouble.

After the visit, Angel got wind that a hit had been put out on him by P Legend's brothers. The hit was for somebody to slice Angel's face. Angel took it up with his advisors, whom he liked to call the Cuban Council. The very next morning, Angel went to the yard. It was a very cold morning, and yard was mandatory for everybody that wasn't a Houseman (an inmate that cleans his cell is called a houseman). Angel had his winter gear on— long johns suit, double shirts, sweater, blue uniform, blue uniform jacket, and blue uniform hat. Angel had his low-key wraparound shades, black boots, and a razor blade in his mouth; he already knew that he could get through the metal detector without setting it off.

Outside on the yard, one of the old-timers was anxiously waiting by the bathroom. Angel met with him, and he handed Angel two shanks. Angel gripped the shanks and wrapped and tied them to his hands like the old-timers taught him. Like a fighting cock, Angel came out of the bathroom with his spurs cuffed in the pocket of his jacket. The old-timers offered to accompany him, but Angel refused and insisted on going alone; they had helped enough.

Angel walked over to the hut where six of P Legend's brothers were sitting holding a meeting. Angel walked up on them, positioning himself so he could face each one.

"Excuse me. I don't mean to rudely interrupt, but this is a life-or-death situation," Angel coldly stated. Some looked with a furrowed brow, while others nervously smiled.

The new ringleader was present and knew Angel from Miami. He asked, "What's going on, brah? Speak your mind."

Angel asked, "Who put the hit out to slice my face?"

They looked at each other, surprised. The ringleader asked his brothers if anybody put a hit out without his authorization, and they all shook their heads no. Then he said, "I didn't put no hit out. Who told you this?"

Angel smirked his crooked smile. "Little bird put it in my ear but check this out: if any one of you have a problem with me or how I handle myself, totally speak up. I told you all Poocho would get dealt with after I got this visit with my mom and family. I don't mean to sound like a mama's boy, but I gave her my word that I would stay out of trouble, so we could spend Christmas together, because I'm her only son and just got a life sentence and have brought so much grief on her that I wanted to make her happy. But who cares about that? That's my personal problems. If any one of y'all has a problem with me and want my face slice, don't send a hit; be a man, and do it yourself!" Angel spit the blade out of his mouth onto the pavement at their feet. Through the shades Angel could see their eyes focusing on the pockets of his jacket. The reality of how serious the situation had gotten dawned on them. They sat still. The slightest movement could trigger a bomb.

Then the ringleader spoke. "You are tripping, Angel . We never sent out a hit. We know how close you and P Legend was. We got love for you, homie. Don't nobody here want to slice your face, so whoever your source is, I don't know where they're getting their info, but they got it all wrong."

Just then Eric (who represented the Latin Kings) walked up with the leader of the Bloods, Hitman. They both let it be known that if Angel got touched, it would mean an all-out war. Angel made it clear that Poocho would get dealt with; he gave them his word. Angel then asked Eric to pick up the blade, and they left.

Not even a week later, Poocho got the left side of his neck sliced by a double blade coming off the rec yard. To this day they don't know who did it.

Angel continued his insanity and addiction with Big Laz. Sherry Angel 's New Girlfriend was coming to see him, bringing treats every now and then. Angel learned how to make "red rooster" (prison wine), and he was getting high and drunk on regular basis. Then when there wasn't any more, Angel would go through his depression, but even worse than his depression was his "numb" days. Those were days when he felt his very existence was meaningless, worthless; he felt like he was dead. They say prison for lifers is like a cemetery of the living dead, and that was how Angel felt on those numb days, like a walking, talking dead man. I saw there was emptiness deep down inside that Angel could not feel. No matter how much drugs or alcohol he consumed, when it was all said and done, when the high or inebriation was gone, the void remained.

On one of those numb days, Angel just happened to be hanging out with one of his homeboys who turned out to be a tattoo artist. Sitting there in silence, bored, feeling numb. Pusher, the tattoo artist, snapped out of the trance. "What's up? Are you going to let me pattt you up?"

Angel said, "F—— it, why not? Might as well. I already got life."

Angel fell in love with the pain. Anything was better than that treacherous numbness. Exterior pain took his concentration away from the emotional and mental pain. It was an escape, and then, after hours or sometimes days of torturous, tormenting pain, it was finished and a beautiful work of art that would last a lifetime became part of his body. Then it was on to the next project. Every time it was a different high—like the relief that cutters experience every time they cut themselves. Every time I visited, it seemed as if Angel had a new tattoo. I only begged that he wouldn't get his face or neck done. He gave me his word. He had a whole back piece, and his arms, chest, and stomach were done. Incredible!

Then one day out of the blue, Sherry left Angel . She'd been cheating on him, but her excuse was that he had too much time, he might never get out, and he was too far away. She just couldn't take it anymore, so she broke like the rest, breaking Angel 's heart. In Angel 's eyes, he had lost it all now that Sherry was gone. He felt hopeless, alone, abandoned by everybody he loved. Angel didn't stop to realize that he had two loves that would never abandon him: God and little ol' me, Mom's love. These two loves are sufficient and long suffering enough to pull him through it all.

CHAPTER 14

Last Woman Standing, Rock-Bottom Remorse, and Redemption

They say it's when you are at your worst, at your most down and out, that you know who truly loves you unconditionally. Proverbs 14:20 says, "A poor man is even hated by his neighbor, but the rich man has many friends." Everybody loves you when you got the money, cars, fancy clothes, extravagant house, power, and so forth and so on. But when you fall and lose it all, how many will be left standing by your side? Sometimes the main people you believe in are the first to fade away, and the people you least expect step up to the plate. There is the cliché many people use: "You keep your friends close, but you keep your enemies closer." Most of the time, it's your own inner circle that smiles in your face but will heartlessly stab you in the back if given the opportunity.

One of Angel 's favorite prayers is "God, protect me from my friends; I can take care of my enemies." It's easy to protect yourself from known enemies. It's the unseen enemy, the unexpected treason of a friend or family member, that hurts the most.

The world was slipping away out of Angel 's grasp, until it finally slipped free, like the string of a helium-filled balloon slipping out of a child's hand and slowly floating away. I was there for Angel 's visiting hours, reminding him how much his family loves him. I got money on the phone for Angel so that if he ever felt lonely or wanted to know about what was going on in the outside world, he was only a phone call away.

Every month I would send him letters so that he'd get something when the officers called mail call, and I'd visit Angel every two months. We had great times together, and even when he was having bad times, I was there for him. I even dedicated songs to Angel, like "By Your Side" by Sade and "Firework" by Katy Perry. I constantly tried to comfort him in any way I could, but I'm only human, and there were times when I went through my depressions. I had my own problems with my spouse and his family. Plenty of times I needed someone to vent to, and the only one I had was Angel . Being a great listener, he gives good advice and knows how to encourage people.

Times were really hard, though, and you know what they say—when it rains, it pours. I began to take things personally, wondering why God was doing this to me. Was God punishing me by punishing my children? I'd been good, I'd been working my program of recovery and had been sober for approximately seventeen years by God's grace. I'd been a faithful believer and servant of God. I had vigorously worked to better myself and please God. So, what was God punishing me for? Why was He allowing all of this to happen?

I was crying my heart out to Angel over the phone one night. It was all just too overwhelming. First my oldest daughter's firstborn could die. Then Angel, my one and only son, was in prison with a sentence of life plus sixty years. It grieved Angel to his soul to hear me in this condition. Trying to cheer me up, he said, "God is not punishing you, Mom. Things just happen sometimes, you know? Don't beat yourself up about it. It's not your fault that this happened to me. I knew what I was getting into. Let's give thanks to God that I got this instead of the other outcome, which is death. I don't know why baby Nathan is going through what he's going through, but I highly doubt God's the cost of it, or any of this, Mom, and let's be real—we just got to be patient. Look at the bright side. My appeals are just getting started. The appeal attorney just requested the trial transcripts, so this isn't over. Baby Nathan was supposed to die when he was three months, and he didn't; he's still alive. So just calm down, please. You know I don't like to hear you cry like this." Angel sighed. "I wish there was something I could do to cheer you up, make you happy."

Then I replied, "You know what could make me happy?"

Angel asked, "What?" I'll do it, whatever it is. You are all I got left in this world; you've done so much for me. I'll do anything you want. How can I help you?"

"Go to church, and pray for me, your nephew, and yourself. I would love that, and it will make me happy."

Angel snorted a chuckle. "Come on, Mom. Are you serious? The last time I went to church at the MetroWest county jail was to catch an enemy of mine. I threw him down the stairs and broke his wrist, forearm, and ankle, and I chipped my tooth in the process. Besides, I've already explained to you that in here going to church is viewed as weakness. They even have this saying, 'If you're scared, go to church,' so what would I look like going to church?"

I responded by saying, "Well, you just asked what will make me happy, and I told you."

Angel laughed. "Fine, Mommy. I give you my word as a man I'll be in church tomorrow morning since it will be Sunday. I don't care what nobody thinks or says about me. I'll pray for the whole family and myself."

I thanked Angel, and the phone operator said we had a minute left, so we said our good-byes and good nights, exchanged our I love you and blew kisses through the phone, and we ended our phone call.

As soon as Angel hung up the phone, he went to his room and smoked a joint with Big Laz. Angel was sitting on the bottom bunk, which was empty because he didn't have a roommate. His mind was racing. Angel 's vision was stuck as if he was frozen. Trying to bring himself back into the room, Angel rubbed his face with his hands, trying to snap out of it, but it was inevitable that Big Laz would notice, and he asked, "What's up? Everything all right? Did you get bad news?"

"Nah, the old girl was just going through it again. She was crying. Everything that's been happening is really taking a toll on her, and when she hurts, I hurt. I'm just sick and tired of being sick and tired. My pain runs so deep that this sh—— (referring to weed) don't even get me high anymore. Something's got to give, homie. Something's got to give. I gave her my word that I was going to go to church tomorrow," Angel told the Big Laz.

Big Laz sighed and then said, "I feel you, Angel . I'll go with you tomorrow to church. I ma leave you alone. Just relax, and I'll see you tomorrow." Big Laz got up and patted Angel on the shoulder on his way out of the cell.

Angel rolled his cell door shut and sat back down, put his head in his hands, and whispered to himself. "Damn. How the f——— did I end up in prison with a life sentence? What in the world have I gotten myself into?"

Angel just sat there in disbelief as his thoughts raced, rushing memories into his mind, visions projecting around his head of that mature man who lectured him in the county jail, the statistics the old-timers told him, me crying and hugging myself in that court after he lost his trial. Visions of his nightmare with the zombies and the dream with Aunt Lea pouring this syrupy blood on his hands, visions of the jury reading the guilty verdict, the judge sentencing him to life plus thirty plus thirty, and the old-timers saying, "You are going to die in prison...prison...prison," and there it echoed to an end. Angel took a deep breath, then slowly exhaled.

Slowly shaking his head from side to side, Angel began to think about all the things he would never do if he had to spend his life in prison. He would never drive a car again, never be able to lie with a woman on a bed. For the rest of his life, he would have to sleep on that uncomfortable mat and eat the food out of the chow hall. Eventually his mother would die, and then there would be no more phone, no more commissary, no more visits. His one and only companion would be gone. Angel grieved just thinking about having to live without his mom's love in such a cold world. I was all he had left. Rewinding the tape of his life, he had to figure out his problem, the root of this problem that led up to all the events that ended in this tragedy. Then he figured it out: as a child, Angel had despised drugs and drug dealers because of what they did to his parents, but he had become the epitome of what he despised the most.

It hit Angel like a sack of bricks. Now he understood that the zombie nightmare represented all the lives he had ruined. Angel was disgusted with himself. He despised himself and was ashamed of himself. Statistically speaking, drugs and alcohol are the major factor in approximately 95 percent of incarcerated individuals. Either they were under the influence of drugs and alcohol when they committed the crime, or they committed the crime to get money to be able to achieve intoxication. Drugs and alcohol belong to an underworld of darkness. Satan has many tools, and drugs and alcohol are the handles to each tool, making your temple (mind, body, and soul) vulnerable to evil spirits and then leaving your door open for the evil spirits to come in and utilize you as their vehicle. These spirits have different names: rape, murder, armed robbery, child abuse, child molestation…and the list goes on.

It is said that the majority of criminal's act on impulse while under the influence. There have been cases of people blacking out only to regain consciousness inside the jail cell. Many men continue in their addictions and insanity even though they are incarcerated. Then there are cases where, through a divine intervention, they rehabilitate themselves, achieving sobriety and experiencing a spiritual awakening, seeking to better themselves. It's like rebooting a computer. They begin to see life through new eyes and build a relationship with God. They evolved into a completely different creature, only to wake up and realize that they're serving time for a crime some other crazy man committed. It's like a shock wave, a complete transformation from one man to another, an exorcism.

> For we wrestle not against flesh and blood, but against principalities, against the rulers of the darkness of this world, against spiritual wickedness high places. (Eph. 6:12)
>
> Being confident of this very thing, that he which hath begun a good work in you will continue it until the day of Christ Jesus. (Phil. 1:6)
>
> Therefore, if any man be in Christ, he is a new creature: old things are passed away; behold all things are become new. (2 Cor. 5:17)

This divine intervention is called redemption. It's rare, and for Angel it came from a special source: his new best friend.

> Behold, I stand at the door and knock: if any man hears my voice and opens the door, I will come in and will dine with him and he with me. (Rev. 3:20)
>
> He has rescued us from the domain of darkness and brought us into the kingdom of the son whom he loves. In him we have redemption the release of sins. (Col 1:13–14)

CHAPTER 15

His New Best Friend

The lights went out. It was bedtime, and Angel lay on his bunk, looking up at the ceiling. How much he wished that morning of mourning never took place.

The next morning Angel met with Big Laz, and they went to church. It was a small crowd, approximately fifty people. The institution's chaplain was preaching the sermon. His father had just died so the chaplain preached about the next life, heaven's paradise, a.k.a. God's kingdom. The chaplain taught that according to scripture, if you believe in your heart and confess with your mouth that Jesus, God's beloved son, died for your sins and was then resurrected on the third day, you will be saved and given God's gift: eternal life (Rom. 10:9, 6:23).

Then the chaplain said that he knew where his father was because his father accepted Christ before dying. Then he went on to say how beautiful it would be, after living in this world filled with trials, tribulations, death, despair, and destruction, to be rewarded with an eternity of paradise, reunited with all your loved ones in a place where all God's creations will be peacefully synchronized and in harmony, where the wolf will feed with the lamb, and the lion will eat straw like the ox (Isa. 65:25). It will be world filled with rejoicing and love. The kingdom of God. "Can you imagine?" said the chaplain. Then he played a music video called "I Can Only Imagine," by Mercy Me, a gospel band. As Angel watched the video and heard the music, his mind began to imagine. Since Angel is a cat lover, he imagined playing with a big lion or a tiger, being reunited with his children (it had been two years since he had seen or talked to either of his kids) and being reunited with his family. The idea of a second chance, a second life in paradise after ruining his current life, intrigued Angel with delightful hope.

After the video, the chaplain closed in prayer and announced that they would be showing a movie in the upcoming week called *The Passion of the Christ*, produced by Mel Gibson. Anyone who was interested should simply submit a request on the way out. Angel looked to his side at Big Laz and said, "Quiere que te saque al cine la semana que viene?" (Do you want me to take you to the movies next week?)

Big Laz chuckled. "I heard it's a good movie, plus Mel Gibson produced it. Sure, why not? I'll go. I got nothing else to do."

Angel smiled and said, "That's the spirit, big guy."

Together, they reviewed their comprehension of the service as they walked back to the dorm, and they agreed that it had been an inspiring sermon that revived hope.

A week later Angel, Big Laz, and a handful of other guys went to watch the movie. From the beginning Angel had a knot in his throat. He couldn't explain what was happening to him, why he was suddenly filled with this overwhelming compassion. Then came the scene in the movie when Jesus's brother is trying to get Caridadto Jesus while He's carrying His cross. Caridaddoesn't know if she can continue, when suddenly Jesus comes into view, carrying His cross and surrounded by a yelling mob. Jesus stumbles and falls. Caridadgets a flashback of when Jesus was a toddler and he tripped and fell on the floor. She abruptly stops what she is doing and runs to Jesus.

Angel felt warm water rushing down his cheeks. He was crying like a child. Embarrassed, Angel looked to his left, only to see big Laz crying like a baby. He looked, and the rest of the grown men were crying also. Angel smiled through the tears and then looked back at Big Laz. He noticed Angel looking and said in between his hyperventilating convulsions, "This is all your fault." *Hiccup, hiccup, hiccup.* "You better not tell"—*hiccup*—"nobody."

"I won't if you"—*hiccup, hiccup*— "won't," Angel responded.

Big Laz looked at the chapel orderly and said, "Can we"—*hiccup*— "get some tissue paper, please?"

The orderly speedily fetched some toilet paper for the guys so they could blow their noses and wipe their tears.

When the movie ended, the chaplain said, "If you guys want to get to know this man that made you'll cry better, you should sign up for an upcoming Bible study called Spiritual Foundations. We have a volunteer with degrees in theology that's going to teach the class. It's only five classes, one day a week, and at the end we will give you a certificate, so if you're interested, just sign the clipboard that's going around."

Sure enough, everybody signed up. Angel told big Laz, "I bet my mom would love it if I sent her that certificate."

Those events were the pivotal moments that truly helped establish Angel 's spiritual foundation. That same night after the movie, Angel got on his knees and prayed to God, "Poppa, I'm tired. I come to you all dirty, full of sins, worthless and dead to the world, condemned to a lifetime in the cemetery of the living dead. I've killed and ruined many lives in my insanity. Please forgive me, Lord. I'm sorry You sent Your son to undergo that horrible torture and execution for the sins of the world. I'm sorry You had to experience that, Jesus. I'm sick and tired of being sick and tired. I messed up bad, Poppa. I thought I had control of the wheel, but I wrecked out. I've lost all control. I give up. I put my life in Your hands. I'm the dirty clay; You are the potter. Please mold me into the man You want me to be. Help me quit smoking, give me strength to exercise, do whatever you want with me. I need your help, Poppa. I need you to heal my nephew. If possible, I need you to help me with my situation. This system is like a tyrant; it's a giant that I can't take on by myself. I'm too little, too weak, and don't have enough money. Help me like you helped David defeat Goliath [1 Sam. 17]. Take away my marijuana obsession, and finally, if you don't grant none of this, at least grant me entrance to Your kingdom so that I can be reunited with my loved ones. I believe in You, and I hand over the steering wheel to You. May Your will be done. I just wish to have a relationship with You. Thank You. In the name of Jesus and the Holy Spirit I pray. Amen."

After that prayer, Angel felt a thousand pounds lifted off his shoulders. He was filled with peace, serenity, and hope.

The volunteer teacher really deciphered the Bible like Angel never heard before, dissecting scripture after scripture. The words came alive, leaping out of the book and applying themselves to his life. The teacher explained that the Bible is an instruction manual on how to live life. The five weeks flew by, and Angel got his certificate and was hooked. He signed up for one Bible study after another, he went to church every Sunday, and he even started working out (exercising). God gave Angel the revelation that exercising while you're still smoking is an oxymoron. Building up your health one minute to then deteriorate it the next makes no sense. Slowly but surely after much struggle, he quit buying packs of cigarettes and bought multivitamins instead. He began reading fitness magazines for men and learned how to eat healthy. One day Angel hit a cigarette out of temptation, and it disgusted him. He vomited; his body and spirit rejected it. I talked Angel into going to meetings and joining the same program of recovery that I was in. Angel started going to meetings every Saturday morning. He stayed clean for six months before relapsing. The spirit convicted Angel, and this time he felt disgusted with himself. Sure enough, the relapse helped Angel realize that he had a desire to quit drinking and drugging.

Big Laz also got closer to God, going to church and Bible studies as well. They both stopped hustling in the ticket game, shutting down their whole operation. Big Laz also quit smoking, drinking, and drugging.

They read a book about Christian martyrs of the world. Angel told Big Laz, "All of Jesus's followers were executed because of their beliefs. They seen something that we didn't, Laz! They witnessed something spectacular! A man performing miracles, feeding and healing thousands. Tortured, crucified, and killed. Then they see him resurrect from the dead, dwelled with him, ate with him, and witnessed him ascend into heaven. His impact was so amazingly magnificent that two thousand years later, people still talk about this man all over the world! No doubt in my mind that if I was there and I would have seen all that, they would've had to kill me too, but Jesus told doubting Thomas, 'Thomas, because you have seen me, you have believed. Blessed are they that have not seen and yet have believed' (John 20:29). He was talking about us, Laz! Jesus was talking about us two thousand years later. Sure, the disciples were privileged with the blessing to see; anyone could believe then. But we have the privilege to be more blessed by believing what we haven't seen through faith in the word by the word and vice versa."

Angel remained clean and sober, and he even began memorizing scripture. He knew none of this was of his own doing; he had no control. It was all God. Angel was exercising, reaching peaks he never imagined. He could run longer and faster and with no fatigue. He was doing more push-ups, chin-ups, dips, et cetera, than he ever imagined. He talked to God always, thanking Him for everything. Angel had built a relationship with God. Jesus was his new best friend.

> I can do all things through Christ who strengthens me. (Phil. 4:13)
>
> He giveth power to the faint, and to them that have no might he increased the strength. Even the youths shall faint and be weary, and the young men shall utterly fall: but they that wait upon the Lord shall renew their strength…they shall run and not be weary; and they shall walk and not faint. (Isa. 40:29–31)

Big Laz received great news: the courts granted him his 3.800 motion. After twenty years day for day of incarceration, Big Laz was going back to Miami–Dade County jail for the correction of an illegal sentence. Big Laz was granted credit time served and was released. Was it a mere coincidence that Big Laz was blessed at the same time he gave his life to Christ? I think not. I no longer believe in coincidences. I believe in God, the creator of time's perfect timing.

Big Laz and his mother came to visit me while I was at work one day. It filled me with emotion to see him reunited with his mother after twenty years. I pictured Angel coming out, a grown, clean-cut, mature man of God. I couldn't help it, I cried and embraced them both. We hugged and talked. Big Laz and his mother assured me that God would make a way. I had faith and I believed. Their visit invigorated me.

Angel continued in his journey. Besides spiritual foundations, Angel also achieved certificates in Survival Kit, Financial Peace University, Anger Resolution, Freedom from Bondage, Free at Last, Origins of Men: Creation vs. Evolution, Small Business Concepts, life Mapping, Wellness, Great Dads Seminar, Bridge Builders, Celebrate Recovery, and Experiencing God. He continued bettering himself in every aspect: spiritually, mentally, emotionally, and physically. He engaged in prayer and meditation daily with his new best friend. Angel began to taste "the fruit of the spirit: love, joy, peace, long suffering, gentleness, goodness, faith, meekness, temperance [self-control]: against such there is no law" (Gal. 5:22–23). Angel began to feel complete. The void within him had been filled by his new best friend. All his life, Angel pursued happiness, looking in all the wrong places. He chased it through drugs and alcohol, only to discover it within the fruit of the spirit, a natural high that rejuvenates itself. God's love is like no other, and Angel couldn't get enough. He wanted more. The more he sought, the more he built, and the more he built, the more Angel wanted to seek. "But without faith it is impossible to please him: for he that cometh to God must believe that he is a rewarder of them that diligently seek him" (Heb. 11:6).

CHAPTER 16

Double-Whammy Miracle
of Disappearances:
"Extra! Extra! Read All about It!"

Like a caterpillar during its metamorphosis into a butterfly or piece of coal turning into a diamond, Angel evolved. He completely transformed from one being into a new creation. Like a computer's mainframe rebooted through shock, Angel decided to try living life using his new instruction manual (the Bible). He invited his new best friend (Jesus) into his heart, surrendering and submitting himself to the powers thereof and rebuking Satan.

Jesus said, "The thief cometh not, but for to steal, to kill and to destroy: I have come that they might have life, and that they might have it more abundantly!" Angel was seeing life through new eyes, from a renewed mind's perspective. He was blind but now could see, was lost but now found. He attempted to contact Anastasia to demonstrate his transformation, to prove to her that he was truly and sincerely changed through miraculous divine intervention. She wouldn't even give him an opportunity to speak; she just cursed him out. Angel missed his kids. Three years had passed since he or I had physically seen or talked to the kids. He had already been in prison for two years waiting on his direct appeal. He had a great appellate public defender, a hardworking Jewish man who used to even take Angel's portfolio back home with him to get familiar with the case to prepare for the appeal. All he needed was the trial transcripts to begin the process.

As usual one afternoon, I visited my daughter. They had taken baby Nathan to an out-of-state hospital where they had some of the finest specialists to see what they could do for him. They had done a bunch of tests and sonograms on Nathan and told Julie and Ricardo that they should fly back home with Nathan. The hospital would contact them as soon as the results returned. Then they would proceed from there with the next step.

The time had come. Julie told me the test results. Apparently, the doctors were a bit dumbfounded. After a thorough observation and screening of everything, it appeared that baby Nathan was going to be okay. According to the doctors, the cysts in Nathan's kidneys had disappeared! The doctors couldn't explain it, but that was fine. We didn't need a thorough explanation, because we all knew that God healed baby Nathan. We were filled with joy! Baby Nathan was going to be okay, and that was all that mattered.

Approximately three hours after I left Julie's house, I was in my condo happy as can be, when suddenly, I got a phone call. It was Angel's appellate public defender. He told me that Angel's trial transcripts had disappeared. What happened was that the stenographer at Angel's trial had run out of paper, so she recorded the whole trial electronically on a disc or USB chip. After the eight-day trial, the stenographer took the records home and tried to transfer the data onto her computer to make copies, but the computer caught a virus. Some technicians were hired to try and salvage the corrupted data, only to have the computer crash, rendering the eight-day trial transcripts "forever lost."

Still on the phone, I asked, "Well, what does that mean?"

The attorney responded, "Apparently, your son is extremely lucky. The odds of that happening are one in a million. That's automatic reverse and remand for a new trial. Angel should consider playing the lotto!" The attorney chuckled at the end.

I had to grab my chest. This was incredible! My heart was skipping beats. I thanked the lawyer, and we said our good-byes. I instantly dropped to my knees and cried tears of joy to God. I thanked Him repeatedly. That was not a mere coincidence! That was God's grace! What a confirmation of God's love—wow! Just then, my phone rang again, and it was Angel. I relayed all the good news to him, and he was shocked with happiness, struck with awe at God's almighty power. The actual experience of God's mighty hand at work was extremely humbling. Amazing grace!

After the phone call, Angel returned to his cell, put a curtain up for privacy, knelt on his knees, and praised God. Thanking Him! Nothing in this world could ever convince him that there wasn't a God.

The proper briefs and motions were filed. The courts tried to reconstruct eight days' worth of trial transcripts, which was impossible, because once God says and does something, it's done! Angel's public defender put up a great fight, and with God's favor he dominated the courtroom. Angel had a right to an appeal after a guilty verdict, and without the actual transcripts, Angel couldn't have a properly lawful appeal. Though reluctant to do so, finally, after Angel had spent a total of two and a half years waiting in prison, the third District Court of Appeals reversed and remanded the original decision. Angel would get a new trial. On New Year's Eve of 2011, I was on the phone with Angel and informed him that the court order to pick him up and bring him back to Miami–Dade County jail was already in. It was official. What a beautiful way to close the year. I will never forget that day and receiving the news concerning the double-whammy miracle of disappearances. I don't think anyone in our family will ever forget it.

After that phone call, Angel returned to his cell again filled with gratitude. He knelt before God in prayer, praising and thanking Him. He ended his prayer with, "May You get all the glory, Poppa."

On January 1, 2012, the very next morning, I went to church. It was a beautiful Sunday service. As soon as church was over, I was getting into my car when I got a call from Victoria's ex-husband.

"Hey, caridad! Have you read the paper?" he said.

"No, why?" I asked, confused.

"Your son, Angel, just made the *Miami Herald*!" he exclaimed.

"No way! Really? Oh, my God!"

We laughed and talked over what had happened. Reporters apparently were enticed by the odds of that happening. I rushed to the first newspaper dispenser I could find and bought one in English and Spanish. There it was, I found it! A local Spanish newspaper even provided a picture of my son. I told the whole family, and I even went out and bought a couple more papers. Out of curiosity, I googled Angel's name. Sure enough, it had been printed all over the world—Australia, Japan, England, Brazil, in the *New York Times*, et cetera.

Angel called me that morning to wish me a happy New Year's Day. I told him about the newspaper, and he was ecstatic. He told me how he had just prayed to God last night. We laughed and marveled at God's mysterious ways. At that moment, I knew that God was working in Angel 's life and that Angel 's testimony would help many people who felt trapped in darkness or imprisoned by sin or who felt they were too bad or evil and that God could never forgive them or love them enough to make an unbelievable transformation in their lives. Well, I got news for the whole world! Whenever you are feeling lonely, abandoned, trapped by sin, in the bondage of addiction, or in helpless trials and tribulations that make salvation seem impossible; when you are trapped where doom, devastation, despair, and death seem inevitable or imminent, I just want you to know that there is one who has conquered the world (John 16:33), who can make the "impossible" for man possible (Luke 18:27) and can make miraculous transformations like He did for Peter and Paul, just to name a few. He makes all things new (Rev. 21:5). He forgives the sins of the world, saving all (John 3:17). The artist of makeovers, the redeemer, the renovator, undefeated, undisputed, king of kings: Jesus Christ (Yeshua, the Messiah).

God had a plan when he chose Paul, because, you see, God knew that the world would be overwhelmed by sin and that governments would have to create a place to cast bad people (sinners); that place would be called prison, jail, or an institution. God knew that the government would institutionalize these places because there would be accumulated masses of "bad people," and thus many more prisons, jails, and institutions would have to be constructed. God knew that these sinners would feel like they were too bad for God's forgiveness, that they were unworthy of God's love, mercy, and grace. God chose Saul, whom he miraculously transformed into Paul (Acts 9:1–22), as an example, a role model for all to see that no matter how many atrocious sins you have committed, God still loves you, God will forgive you, and God will save you and give you a life more abundant (John 10:10). He will free you from addictions, alcoholism, a life of crime, poverty, sickness, and even death by granting eternal life (Rom. 6:23). If God did it for Paul, Angel, and so many more, he can do it for you too; you just must let him. Accept God into your life and be amazed. God even used Paul to write twelve books of the Bible, possibly thirteen, and Paul wrote them all from inside prison.

CHAPTER 17

Back on a Fluke, Temptations, and Angel's First-Year Medallion

While waiting for Miami–Dade County to come pick him up, Angel began preparing himself for his return. There were a couple of older guys, Mickey and Bundy, who Angel was hanging out with and who were lifers as well. They offered him some advice.

Mickey told him, "Angel, listen to me, little brother. When you get back, don't play with them people; if they offer you that same twenty-five-year plea, take it! I've done twenty-eight years already, I'm forty-eight years old, and look at me. I don't look old, I still play ball, I work out, and Lord knows if I could get out there right now, I'd be f**** like a jackrabbit."

Angel laughed, pressed his lips and nodded his head in agreement. (Truth be told, Mickey still looked like a teenager; prison had preserved him, but he wasn't trying to hear that. He believed and hoped that his plea bargain would go down, ranging from ten to fifteen years with some probation.)

Bundy said, "You've been blessed. You're getting a chance neither of us might never receive. God willing, they'll bring back the plea bargain. I urge you to truly consider taking it, because a release date really makes a difference. You're young; hopefully you'll make it out to your mom before she dies. You could be there for her in her old age, provide for her, and even hold her hand when it's time to cross over to the other side of her life. Think about her. Think about having to live in prison without her, because as time goes by, she will eventually die. It's only getting harder and harder in here to get by without outside support. My mom and dad passed away while I was on this bid. I should have been home, but I let my ego get the best of me, and I didn't take the plea deal. Now look at me, stuck without an "L" bow (Life sentence). I've been fighting the system for eighteen years now. So, don't be foolish, don't play with them, and I wish the best for you."

Angel couldn't have been happier to be coming back home, but profoundly he knew all too well that a lot of old demons awaited him with arms wide open.

The ride back home was torturously inhumane. Angel and ten other men were crammed into an all-steel paddy wagon, shoulder to shoulder, like sardines in a can. To make matters worse, there wasn't any air conditioning. He said it was cruel and unusual punishment.

Finally, after two and a half years, Angel was back in the pretrial detention center (the Jungle), but the Jungle had changed. The county installed surveillance cameras in all the cells, and officers were assigning people to bunks. The tradition of fighting upon entering the cell had changed. The cameras could detect fast motions, signaling the observing officers to the cell and thus making unnoticed rec or paint sessions impossible.

Angel ran into a lot of old acquaintances. Most them had gotten out to the streets only to violate probation within the first couple of months of being free and return with new charges. Angel met many new faces—a lot of young men eighteen, nineteen, or twenty years old with punishable-by-life (PBL) charges. The county was now charging five dollars a day, making it impossible to order from the canteen. I never understood how they could charge people who weren't even working. In all actuality, the county was charging the families or loved ones.

The officers assigned Angel to a lower bunk. He continued his morning time with God, kneeling to pray, reading the Bible and daily devotionals. He shared his testimony with almost the whole cell; some heard, and others didn't care to hear. Angel's court-assigned attorney came to see him. This was the same man who had lost the first trial; he would be representing him again. They talked for a little bit, Angel got bad vibes, and that was that.

His first court appearance was just to make sure that he was present at the pretrial detention center. Angel's very next court date was strictly business. The judge wanted to know how soon they could start the new trial and if there was any plea deal available. Though the judge was different, Angel had received the same vindictive prosecutor, and her response to the judge was, "Your Honor, this is a simple open-and-shut case. The defendant is back on a fluke. We've already got a conviction. The victim's family has already suffered enough. We have no plea bargain for the defendant. We're ready for trial, and we seek a second conviction so that we can get this over with and send the defendant back to where he came from with his life sentence."

The judge looked over to the defense table and asked Angel's lawyer if he was ready for trial. He replied that he wasn't. "Your Honor, I need a continuance."

The judge asked, "Why? If you were ready for the first trial, you should be ready now. This is a seven-year-old case."

"Well, Your Honor, I'm developing a strategy. I want to proceed from a different angle."

The prosecutor said, "He doesn't have a new strategy. He's going to use the same defense."

Referring to the prosecutor, the defense attorney said, "Your Honor, she doesn't know what I'm preparing. She's not psychic or a mind reader!"

The judge chuckled along with the prosecutor. They didn't take this guy seriously; he was a joke. The judge gave the defense attorney a two-month continuance.

Angel was discouraged. This was not what he'd been expecting. After everybody left the courtroom for a break, Angel looked at me and said, "This dude's a clown, Ma. He's weak. If I'm ever going to win trial or even get a good deal, it isn't going to be with his representation. He sucks, and as long as the prosecutor is confident of winning, why should she bring a plea deal?"

After two and a half years of not having the pressures of a court appearance, Angel was truly overwhelmed with the whole situation. I called Big Laz and asked for advice. He advised that I should hire a real-deal private attorney like the one who got him out. I ran the idea by Angel. I told him I had $7,000 saved that we'd planned to use to hire an appellate attorney for his 3.850 motion. Angel told me that trial attorneys for murder trials charge a minimum of $25,000. Frustrated, he said he would pray over it but for the meantime I should do some lawyer shopping. There was one lawyer that Angel preferred over all. His name was Andy. At that time, he was infamous for murder trials, so Angel suggested that I pay him a visit as well. I set up appointments and visited a couple of attorneys. A lot of them were familiar with Angel's case. The cheapest price they offered was $25,000 with a down payment of $10,000 up front. Angel asked if I had gone to see the lawyer named Andy. I said no; I didn't think he would be affordable. Angel said to try. Nothing is impossible, and God would provide. So, I set up an appointment. On the day of the consultation, Angel prayed and fasted.

The lawyer Andy had a great personality. Although he usually charged exorbitant fees, he asked what the "other guys" were charging. I told him twenty-five grands. He pressed his lips together, thinking about it, taking it all into consideration. God moved his heart, and he said, "I'll do it for twenty-five grands." He even accepted my $7,000 down payment. I gave Angel the good and bad news. The good news was that we got Andy and his professional association for twenty-five grand, which was what the average joes were charging. Plus, he accepted my $7,000 down payment. The rest was to be paid in weekly installments since we were so pressed for time. Upon Angel's next court date, the court-assigned lawyer would be fired, and Andy and his PA would be hired, thus buying a little more time for the new attorneys to prepare for trial and for me to come up with the rest of the money.

The bad news was that I was eighteen grands short. I had bills and things to pay for, and with the little bit of money I was making at my job, it appeared to be practically impossible! Where in the world was I going to get eighteen grands from? I was exasperated, worried, and scared. Angel chuckled over the phone. "Calm down, Mom. God has brought us this far; He will provide. You're not alone. You're smart, so just be attentive, and God will show you the way."

That night after the phone call, Angel knelt before his bottom bunk and prayed, "Oh, Heavenly Father, I come before Your throne once again as humble as I know how. Please forgive me for my sins. I just want to thank You for bringing me this far, but Lord, we need better representation. This court-assigned dude sucks! Poppa, I got one of the best now—besides you, of course. He is charging twenty-five grands. My mom paid seven grand, but she's eighteen grands short. Poppa, I know You live in paradise, in a kingdom with riches untold. You are creator and ruler of all. I need You to give me or loan me eighteen grand, Poppa. Help my mom get this money, please. I can't do much, but I will fast one day every week until my mom gets the rest of this money. I believe in You, and I have faith! I trust You to make a way! I love You. Good night, Poppa. Thanks again. Amen."

Angel kept his word and started fasting for twenty-four hours straight every Tuesday. Meanwhile I was praying constantly, Then the devil began throwing temptations at Angel . One morning at about four o'clock, Angel was rudely interrupted out of his sleep. Some new guy had entered the cell and decided to challenge Angel for his bottom bunk. Angel woke up to a multiple-choice question: fight or give up the bottom bunk. Angel fought and lost, but neither one of them got the bunk because the new cameras alerted the officers, who moved Angel and his adversary to different cells. Angel got moved into a cell that just so happened to turn into an honor cell a week after he had been moved there. They received special privileges like "contact visits" and extra rec yard time. If the cell was clean, the bunks were made up prison style, and there weren't any fights, they kept their privileges. I mean, what are the odds? That isn't coincidence or dumb luck; that's Gods favor.

Now Angel got the chance to enroll himself in a vocational trade: environmental services and entrepreneurship skills. It was four days a week, every week, for approximately three months. Angel studied hard and went to every class.

It was kind of difficult to concentrate with the stress of court dates, preparing for trial, and nonsense in the cell. Not to mention the temptations of relapse. With so much weed circulating all through the county, it would have been so easy to just say, "The hell with it all. I need to release some stress, get high, and relax." Angel was in the cell with a childhood friend and plenty of new acquaintances who freely offered him a chance to smoke. But as tempting as it was, Angel was trying to stay true to his program of recovery. He was only two months away from his first one-year medallion. Angel stayed in the word but never lost his characteristics. Angel still had a cool attitude and a great sense of humor. He made people laugh, helped bring peace at times of uprising, but continued staying focused on his school, case, program of recovery, and relationship with God.

Out of his class of twenty men, only four graduated. Out of a facility that holds approximately one thousand men, only four men wished to truly better themselves with determination, discipline, and persistence. They persevered, passing five state exams and a buffer machine test, taking over sixty hours of training, and educating themselves. Four men out of a thousand; that's less than 1 percent. My son, Angel, was one of those men. He scored highest in his class and was the valedictorian. Angel prepared and read a speech that filled everyone with compassion, even moving his teacher to tears. My son accomplished his first-ever state-certified vocational trade. He also accomplished his first full year being clean and sober since the age of ten and was awarded his first one-year medallion in his twelve-step program of recovery. I had the honor of presenting it to him. We spent a wonderful time together at the graduation. Angel invited me and Mima, and we were so proud.

While he was incarcerated, Angel earned his GED / high school diploma, learned a vocational trade, and earned an abundance of other certificates. If that's not proof of a miraculous transformation through divine intervention, then I don't know what is.

But God's abounding mercy, grace, and blessings in Angel 's life weren't done just yet. Eighteen grands had to appear from somewhere, and something had to happen in the courtroom. Angel 's case had to be resolved someway, somehow.

CHAPTER 18

All His Angels and the Light at the End of the Tunnel

Giving what little we had to the lawyer, we stepped out in the water with blind faith and without a clue as to how we would acquire the remaining $18,000 we owed. As Angel put it best, "Unlike Peter, we will not look down to the water with doubt. We will keep our focus on Jesus."

Angel continued his fasting one whole day every week, and on that day, he would focus on the word all day long, praying and meditating for God to provide for me, for God to show me the way. I didn't panic or get hysterical. I remained cool, calm, collected, and attentive. Then out of nowhere, my husband Ernie gave me one hundred dollars for Angel 's attorney. "That's it!" I thought. "I'll make a list of everybody I know, explain to them the situation, and ask them if are willing to donate one hundred dollars or whatever they can spare to help Angel ." I made a list of people I knew and people who knew Angel —his so-called "friends." The worst that could happen was that they would say no, and I'd end up back at the drawing board. Regardless, I had nothing to lose simply by asking. "Ask, and it will be given to you. Seek, and you will find. Knock, and the door will be opened to you" (Matt. 7:7). I figured if I could make a list of one hundred people or more, I could at least get between $5,000 and $10,000. That would surely be a blessing.

Amazingly, it worked; money began to flow in. July's Jehovah's Witness congregation even helped donate a large sum, and my twelve-step program of recovery came together, donating a great contribution as well. People I had least expected to contribute freely cooperated, giving me a hundred bucks here and a hundred bucks there. It was unbelievable that everybody was willing to help me and Angel .

One of the young ladies that I sponsor in the twelve-step program came up with a wonderful idea of throwing a picnic in a park, charging an entrance fee, doing raffles, and feeding hot dogs to the crowd. All proceeds would go to pay Angel's attorney. We planned it out and did it. My whole family came together, and all my friends from the twelve-step program came. Julie, Ricardo, and a lot of their congregation participated as well. The entrance tickets were ten dollars apiece. All the women in Angel's life at that time wore matching shirts that read "Mom's love picnic."

Out of nowhere this man showed up with ponies for the children to ride for a fee. Apparently, he was there for some birthday party but happened to arrive a couple of hours early, so with time to spare, he decided to make a few bucks at our picnic. He was also giving the kids treats that he had. Nathan and his new kid sister enjoyed themselves riding the ponies along with other kids that were at the picnic. Some people were throwing football in the background. My family and I served hot dogs to the guests, music was blasting in the air, and then we did the raffle. Grace had donated a Movado watch to be raffled off, and the raffle tickets went for five dollars. We had a pair of mountain bikes donated by Victoria. Christina's boyfriend at the time owned a beauty school, so he donated a variety of gift certificates for hairdos, manicures, pedicures, and massages for the raffle.

Not only did we make a lot of money that day, but we also had a spectacular time. What a beautiful day! The sun was shining, the sky was a clear blue, and the cold winds were refreshing. Such a wonderful, precious moment at a picnic in a life-filled park in Miami. Just the right remedy to relieve some stress, get away from the madness, and simply enjoy some good, clean fun. At the end of the day, we kept the money that was donated and took it to the lawyer the next day.

I also sold chocolate and candy at my job, just to make some extra money on the side. In three months the lawyer was paid off, just in time for the new trial. My mother donated $5,000 on a credit card, and the remaining balance of $18,000 balance was paid off. To this day I still marvel at that experience. Wow! God provided incredibly! I'd never accumulated that much money so fast before in my life. It was as if God had sent His angels to provide for Angel and me. All our ideas worked! But of course, they were inspired by God, so how could they fail? Angel was filled with joy and gratitude and was humbled by God's majesty once again.

The attorneys worked with vigorous efforts to prepare for trial. The real battle was just getting ready to take place; the battlefield was really in that courtroom. The time for trial had arrived; this was it, the moment of truth, crunch time. As I walked into the courtroom with Angel's shirt and shoes, I had a knot in my stomach and the weight of the world on my shoulders. I felt as if an elephant was sitting on my chest and butterflies were flopping around inside of me. I wasn't alone; I had both of my daughters, Julie and Christina, with me, my boyfriend Ernie, and my sponsor. I was scared. I felt as if this whole nightmare was just replaying itself all over again. I didn't know how much more of this I could possibly endure.

To my left sat the victim's family. I could feel their cold stares. I walked over and handed the clothes to Angel's attorney, who took it into a back room, which was the jury deliberation room. We took our seats and patiently waited.

Angel was escorted into the courtroom. My baby boy was clean cut and looking sharp. I felt a knot in my throat. "Okay, here we go," I thought. "I got to be strong for him." I smiled at him, and he smiled back, but I could see his concern, his worry, and his fear. His attorney brought him some papers to read. Angel laughed out loud, looked at me, and held his thumb up. He was bluffing. He looked over to the prosecutor with the most confidence he could possibly muster and gave his smirk as though he knew something they didn't.

The judge entered the courtroom, and all rose and then sat. The judge called Angel's name, and Angel stood up. The judge asked the prosecutor if she had a plea offer. The prosecutor said she did not at the time but would hear out what the defense counterplea sounded like. The defense entered a counterplea of twenty-two years with probation. The prosecutor cut him off, saying that according to the 10-20-Life law, she couldn't go under twenty-five years' mandatory and she didn't even know if the victim's family was willing to go forward with a plea deal. She would need some time to run it by them. The judge called a recess to give the prosecutor time to speak with the victim's family.

In the meantime, Angel was fighting his own battles within. He knew that he couldn't win at trial, and his attorney entering a counterplea of twenty-two years confirmed his heart's fear. He was also concerned with my reaction if he were to lose at trial again. Twenty-five years is a lot of time; his whole youth would be spent in prison, and he would be out at the age of forty-five. Angel was tormenting himself, so many thoughts rushing through his head.

Angry, frustrated, agitated, and overwhelmed Angel started to cry. This was not what he had expected. He'd figured this would all get resolved with a reasonable plea. Then Angel looked over at me. In Spanish he said, speaking more to the victim's family than to me, "For the love of God, I never wanted problems with this man or his family. He came to my home; I defended myself. Why is this family throwing the authorities on me mercilessly as if he was an innocent child, a little angel? How long will this go on? When will they accept the fact that he was a thug just like me? Better yet, if they even think for one second that I will stop fighting this case, they are greatly mistaken. This will go on forever. I will fight until I die. We'll continue with trial if they want trial. If I lose, I'll come back on appeals. We'll continue this rumble, this dance, until at last we can come to an understanding."

Officer Nixon couldn't understand Spanish, but it was evident that Angel was upset and speaking with his mind out loud. He called Angel, asking him to join him in the holding cell out back. Angel complied and was escorted to the holding cell. Just then the prosecutor stepped into the courtroom and asked the victim's family outside into the hallway to run the plea deal by them. Meanwhile Mr. Nixon asked Angel, "What are you going to do?"

Angel replied, pacing back and forth like a tiger in a cage in his orange-and-black uniform, "I don't know! I don't care! I lost my life 2005 along with that dude. I lost everything! They want to go to trial—run that sh——! I'll tell my attorneys to display the most graphic pictures!"

Officer Nixon shook his head side to side in disappointment and said, "Now you see, there you are going back to the old Angel . Son, when you came back from prison, you had a glow, an aura. Something was different about you. Everybody could see it."

Angel snapped out of it. He remembered all his experiences with God, that inner peace he shared with Poppa. He plopped down onto the bench, threw his head in his hands, and bawled like a child, ashamed with his behavior and his reaction to everything. Mr. Nixon continued, saying, "You see, son, things don't go your way, and you have this ability, this habit of blocking everything off, shutting everything out." He motioned with his hands as if he was enclosing his head in a steel-walled box. "Drop that egotistical pride, and think about your family, think about your mom. Try to see light at the end of the tunnel, son." As Mr. Nixon said this, Angel remembered that pride defeats man and humility defeats pride. "You are young. Let's do the math. If they bring back the twenty-five-year plea, you have seventeen years left. You will be forty-five years old. That's younger than me. How old is your mom?"

Angel calmly answered, "Fifty-four years old."

"She'll be seventy-two years old. You get out there and take care of her. Be there for her; she's been here for you. Think about it, man. Don't block and shut everything out; it's not about you anymore. People do things now in days that carry life sentences and expect five, ten, fifteen years. The laws have changed." He held his hands as though they were the two sides of a scale. "Weigh it out: a life sentence or seventeen years. You have life. You were stuck in a dark tunnel, but now God's blessing you with a light at the end of that tunnel."

Angel pressed his lips together and smiled through the tears, nodding his head in agreement.

Mr. Nix then said, "I'm supposed to get your lunch, but I doubt you're going to eat."

"No, thank you. I'm fasting, sir" Angel responded.

Mr. Nix smiled and nodded his head. "Now that's the new Angel I seen come back from prison! I'm leave you alone. Take what I said into consideration, and take it to the Lord in prayer, son." Mr. Nix tapped the iron bars with his keys and walked away.

Angel knelt down and prayed, "Oh God, what do I do? I wish You could speak to me, tell me what to do. Help me, please, and forgive me for going back to my old ways."

Suddenly, Angel remembered a skill that he learned through one of those Bible studies where he'd learned how to listen to God speak through the body of Christ.

"Okay! Thank you, Poppa. You're the best! Oh yeah, in Jesus's name. Amen."

Thirty minutes later Mr. Nix escorted Angel back into the courtroom and then into the jury deliberation room where Angel 's attorneys and the state prosecutor awaited. The prosecutor offered Angel the twenty-five-year plea with five years' administrative probation with early dismissal after two years of good behavior. That was all they had to offer, the only plea available on the table. Angel asked to speak with his family. Mr. Nix sat Angel as close as he could to us. I asked Angel what was going on, and he said, "Well, the only plea on the table is twenty-five years, with administrative probation for five years, but I'll get early termination with good behavior after two years—or go to trial."

I asked Angel, "Well, what are you going to do?"

He replied, "I don't know what to do. This is not about me anymore." He turned to me and the family. "What do you guys want me to do? I'm brave enough to do whatever you want me to do."

We didn't know it at the time, but Angel was applying a skill he'd learned in Bible study while a prison. It goes like this: When a pastor has a decision to make—for example, like moving a church to a different location—and he wants it to be God's will, not his own, the pastor is to take it up with the head of the church, Jesus Christ. Next the pastor is to bring together the congregation (the body of Christ) and present the options. Then they are all to pray, seeking guidance from the head of the church to move the body, and then they each separately and privately write their God-inspired decision on a piece of paper. Finally, they are to come together, and this is where the miracle happens. Nine times out of ten, God will move all their hearts to make the same decision in a near-unanimous vote of approximately 90 percent to 10 percent, given that the 10 percent are not aligned with the will of God for whatever reason; for instance, around this time Angel had gone back with Sherry. Yes, the same chick who cheated on him and abandoned him. She was opposed to any plea. She wanted Angel to fight and go to trial, and she told him that even if he were to lose she wouldn't make the same mistake she made last time in leaving him; she would be there for him.

Julie was the first to say, "Take the plea, Angel . You'll be getting out one day, and forty-five years old is still relatively young. You won't die in prison."

Wow! The elephant lifted off my chest, and the massive weight of the universe was released from my back and shoulders. The knots and butterflies within were replaced with joy, excitement, and relief.

I exclaimed, "Take the plea! I'll be at peace! This way I'll know for sure that if anything happens to me you won't be abandoned to rot and die a miserable death in prison. Please take the plea for me."

Cristina joined in. "Yeah! Take the plea! You'll be out one day."

My sponsor said, "Take the plea, Angel ."

My boyfriend Ernie said in Spanish, "Yeah, take the plea, my son. Every time I had a run-in with the law, I always copped out. That going to trial was insanity on your part."

Angel utilized us as the body of Christ. God spoke to him through us.

Angel remembered all his friends in prison, the old-timers and all the young men with life sentences. All the advice he received from José, Rojas, Big Laz, Eric, Micky, Bondi, and other. Then he applied a slogan from our program of recovery: "Doing the same things and expecting different results is our definition of insanity."

Angel looked at me sincerely and asked, "Is this what you truly want, Mommy?"

"Oh yes, please! I feel it in my heart that this is the right choice. Just the thought of it releases all my stress."

Angel rubbed his face with his hands and went back to the deliberation room, where he asked his attorneys, "Being my lawyers and the experts here, what do you believe is my best interest?"

The lawyer replied, "I can't guarantee a win here, Angel . The only thing I would guarantee is that you'll have a better trial than your first. I've got two of my best attorneys here with me, and we will do our very best to get you self-defense. You made yourself the owner of the drugs. You admitted that they were yours to save your family from incarceration, and I understand that, but it complicates things. Maybe the jury would overlook it, maybe not. If I do get you self-defense, they still might find you guilty on the drugs. Now how much did they give you for that?"

Angel answered, "thirty years plus thirty years equals sixty years."

"Well, that's what it boils down to."

"What about the motion to sever chargers?"

"We could do that." All the attorneys agreed. "Because if we could sever the drugs from the body, then they can't contaminate the jury with prejudice due to the drugs, all within the self-defense case, then cop out to the drugs."

They went forth with the motion to sever, but the judge denied it. Angel took a deep breath and exhaled. He looked over at us next to the victim's family. Then he looked at the prosecutor, his attorneys, and the judge and said, "I'll take the plea."

Angel felt a little demon voice inside say, "But nothing is impossible for God. You could win trial through a miracle." Then he remembered a scripture from the Bible, Matthew 4:6–7, where Satan says to Jesus, "If you are the son of God, throw yourself down. For it is written, he shall command his angels concerning you, and upon their hands they should lift you up, so that you might not strike your foot against a stone," and Jesus says, "It is written, you shall not tempt your God."

To walk by faith does not mean to stop thinking or using sound judgment. Acting foolishly or thoughtlessly, expecting God to bail you out when things go wrong, isn't faith at all. It's presumption and a distortion of biblical faith.

After Angel accepted the plea deal, the judge had to read the conditions of the plea bargain, in addition to asking Angel a series of questions for the record, making sure he clearly understood that he was entering a guilty plea freely and voluntarily in exchange for the plea bargain. Right in the middle of this processes, Angel got the sudden urge to refuse and commence the trial. He looked back at me for strength, and I encouraged him to go on and continue answering the questions by whispering, "Yes. Say yes." He would answer like a reluctant, rebellious child. It was quite comical; he's funny even in a serious situation.

The judge asked, "Is anybody forcing you to enter this plea of guilty?"

Angel looked back at me with contempt, and I smiled, egging him on. "Say no. Say no."

Angel continued the motions of answering the questions, but in his head, he was upset, thinking, "I'm tired of being locked up. I don't want to do this time. I wanted less time."

Suddenly, Angel heard Grace as if she was standing right next to him singing in his ear, taunting and teasing him with the song "You can't... always get what you want. You can't always get what you want! You can't always get what you want! You can't always get what you want!" Angel couldn't help but smile to himself. God does have a sense of humor after all. God is a God of love, mercy, and grace, but He is a just God. Angel wrote a heartfelt letter to everybody that helped and offered their love and support he titled it: To all my angels.

Hebrews 12:2–11 reads,

> Focusing on Jesus the initiator and perfecter of faith. For the joy set before him, he endured the cross, disregarding its shame, and he has taken his seat at the right hand of the throne of God. Consider him who has endured such hostility by sinners against himself, so that you might not grow weary in your souls and lose heart. In struggling against sin, you have not yet resisted to the point of bloodshed. Have you forgotten the warning addressed to you as sons?
>
> My sons do not take lightly the discipline of God or lose heart when you are corrected by him, because God disciplines the one he loves and punishes every son he accepts. It is for discipline that you endure. God treats you as sons, for what son does a father not discipline? But if you are without discipline, something all have come to share, then you are legitimate and not sons.
>
> Besides, we are used to having human fathers as instructors, and we respect them. Shall we not much more be subject to the father of spirits and live? Indeed, for a short time they disciplined us as seemed best to them; but he does so for our best benefit, so that we might share in his holiness. Now all discipline seems painful now, not joyful, but later it yields the peaceful fruit of righteousness to those who have been trained by it.

CHAPTER 19

Change, Recovery and Redemption`

One Year Later

Nowadays Angel leads a new life in Christ, continuously bettering himself across the board. He still does Bible studies, and he participates in holistic activities, going to church on Sundays and attending meetings (twelve-step programs or recovery); he's even served as chairman. He exercises, eats healthy, and remains sober. He got assigned to work on the farm, so he is in tune with his roots, doing what my father and grandfather used to do. Angel loves it. Who would've ever thought? God works in mysterious ways.

He continues his relationship with God, enjoying all of God's creations while working on the farm. He loves watching the red-tailed hawks and watching all other types of birds like cardinals, mockingbirds, and sparrows. Like a kid, he plays with frogs, mice, toads, grasshoppers, and spiders.

He has been blessed with wisdom so that at times of racial wars or gang wars and uprising. Angel sometimes clears up misunderstandings, bringing peace and sharing his testimony with anyone willing to listen. He starts off every morning by reading four daily devotionals: *Daily Reflections, Our Daily Bread, Faith to Faith*, and *God Calling*. That's in addition to spending time in prayer and meditation with the Lord. He ends his nights by reading *Bedside Blessings* and praying. Angel is a completely different man now. He has tried to make amends with Anastasia to no avail.

It's been six years since we've physically seen or talked to the kids, but we'll continue praying for them. Sherry left Angel within his first month of returning to prison, but that's okay because God has blessed him with a godly woman, a beautiful young lady who truly loves him. Her name is Mellie. Her whole family loves him. They write him and even go visit him. Mellie has become his new companion, unlike any girl he ever had.

Sometimes I sit back and am amazed by the transformation that God has made in Angel 's life. What the devil manifested for bad, death, and destruction God turned into good, life, and salvation. I believe God's not done with Angel yet. This is turning him into a farmer, and sometimes he's developed a passion for it—tilling the soil, turning it over, making rows, fertilizing the soil, planting the seeds correctly, watering them and watching God work His magic, then pulling the weeds so they won't choke out the baby plants, and finally watching the baby plants grow and bear fruit and reaping a plentiful harvest.

Matthew 9:35–38 reads,

> Then Jesus went about all the cities and villages, teaching in their synagogues, preaching the gospel of the kingdom, and healing every sickness and every disease among the people, but when he saw the multitudes, he was moved by compassion for them, because they were weary and scattered, like sheep having no shepherd. Then he said to his disciples, "The harvest truly is plentiful, but the laborers are few. Therefore, pray the Lord of the harvest to send out laborers into his harvest."

I pray that this testimony reaches troublesome youths, prisoners, and children of poverty who are weary and scattered like sheep who have no shepherd. May Angel 's life be an exhibit of what a life of crime and drugs can lead to, so that they might avoid decades of heartache and pain. Though Angel seems extremely blessed, he still has a long journey ahead of him. When all of this is said and done, Angel will have spent the best years of his life, practically his entire youth, behind two layers of barbed wire fence. Institutionalized.

My advice to mothers all around the world is to never give up on your children, no matter how hopeless the situation might seem to you at that precise moment. Eventually it will build up momentum like a rolling snowball becoming an avalanche, and it will one day hit them. The satisfaction of seeing your children changing and finally gaining salvation is worth your vigorous efforts.

Verily I say to you, mothers, if there's anything in this world that can give your child a taste of heaven on earth, a sample of God's mercy, grace, and love, I would say it is none other than that good old-fashioned, persevering, long-suffering, unconditional…Mom's love.

THE ACKNOWLEDGMENT

I am grateful to the editors from CreateSpace
for all their help and dedication,
I will like to thank God and the twelve steps program of AA for 24
years of sobriety, I will like to thank my sponsors Carolina, Ada,
Berny. To my spiritual leaders for their words of encouragement.
My mother Alberta for being the best mother ever, my Husband
Ernesto for giving me all the support while this book was completed.
I will like to thank AO that drew the cover for my son
behind bars, and my friend's son Velentino Urroz Mezza for
making it into such a nice painting for the cover page.
I will like to give thanks God for the change in the life of
my son Angel that was able to be this book inspiration, and
for all the blessing in my life and the life of my family.

Printed in the United States
by Baker & Taylor Publisher Services